All That Glitters

J.L. Lynnlee, A.T.T.S.

Schiffer Publishing Ltd

West Chester, Pennsylvania 19380

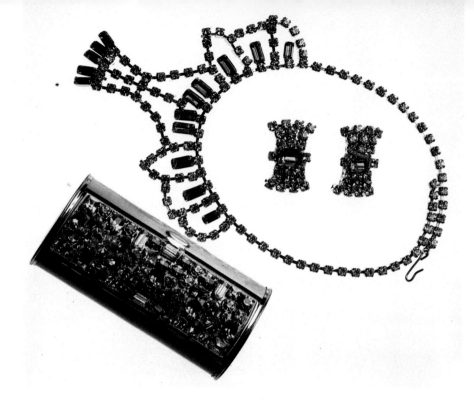

Rhinestone decorated carrying case. Value $25. Shown with drop necklace and matching earrings. Large rhinestones prong set. Value $85 set.

Printed in the United States of America.
ISBN: 0-88740-069-8
Published by Schiffer Publishing Ltd.
1469 Morstein Road, West Chester, Pennsylvania 19380

This book may be purchased from the publisher.
Please include $1.50 postage.
Try your bookstore first.

To Lorraine
whose knowledge is boundless
and whose sharing permits
all around her to grow

Three piece rhinestone set in pinks and reds. Rhinestones multi-faceted and prong set. Earrings demonstrating twin stones, c. 1930. Value $125 set.

Acknowledgments

The author would like to acknowledge the following people for their support and good works throughout the creation of this book. Peter Garcia for interior photos and his friendship. Geoffrey Gross, cover photographer and Karen Kihlstom cover stylist. Lorraine Matt whose days were made topsy-turvy while on the hunt. Karen Johnstone for her continuous supply of glitter. A special thanks must go to Bob Coyle and Denise Wiesner of the Peoples Store, Lambertsville, New Jersey. Ruth Fassell, Betty Martin, Becky Frey, Suzanne Tavella and Kathryn Welch for sharing. Hazel Gutowsky of Trifari for all of her efforts and last but certainly not least Joel, Jami, Josh, Caroline and Flo all of whom seem to be able to read minds.

Table of Contents

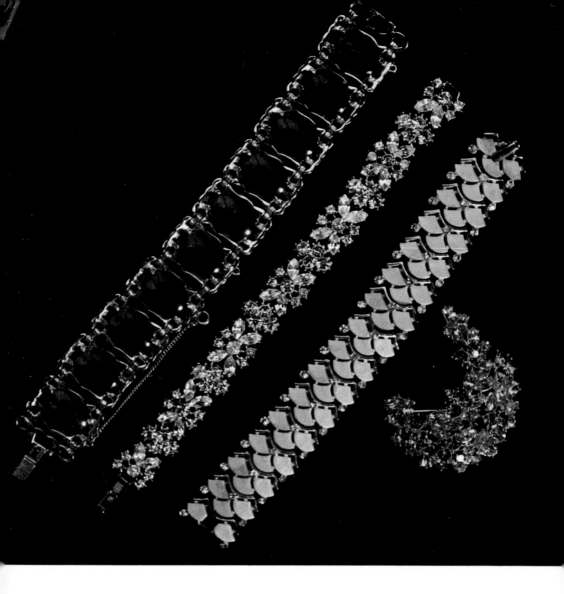

Left to right: All by Trifari; brushed gold bracelet with prong set cranberry glass, cabochon cut and safety chain—$35. Floral design link bracelet with prong set rhinestones—$35. Brushed gold bracelet with prong set rhinestones—$25. Floral spray pin in shades of gold with prong set rhinestones—$25.

Introduction

Costume jewelry of the twentieth century may be viewed as one more phenomenon of the modern world. In its essence, it is a glittering mirror of our times. Reflecting in all of its glitz and glamour are the rapid growing pains of a maturing America, the ingenuity, creativity and true guts of the American dream. Born of imitation, christened with the notion that it couldn't last, entering adolescence with a streak of rebellion that turned the minds of millions to its acceptance, it has matured to stand on its own feet as an art form and trend setter in and of itself.

Jewelry, like furniture, china or architecture, has different periods, but unlike these other art forms, styles and trends of costume jewelry changed not with the decades, but with each new season. By the 1920s the pace of America had picked up. We were galloping toward the future. Styles were here one day and gone the next with many themes returning again and again. It was the beginning of the youth movement, womens' lib and the middle class. The Victorian age with its gloom and alacrity was doomed. The costume jewelry industry was quick to realize our changing society and, taking its lead first from the fashion designers, then turning to the arts for inspiration, it finally combined the two medias to produce in over a 60 year period an awesome amount of decoration.

This book will endeavor to give an overview of affordable costume jewelry and trends down through the decades showing the jewelry in vogue along with the outside stimuli that contributed to the styles. The industry ran the gamut in production from five and ten cent goods all the way to fashion jewelry. The subject of high fashion jewelry has been successfully dealt with in other books. This book intends to deal with the back bone of the industry—jewelry which was available to all at a modest price. It is from this base that the industry survived, broadened its fields and flourished.

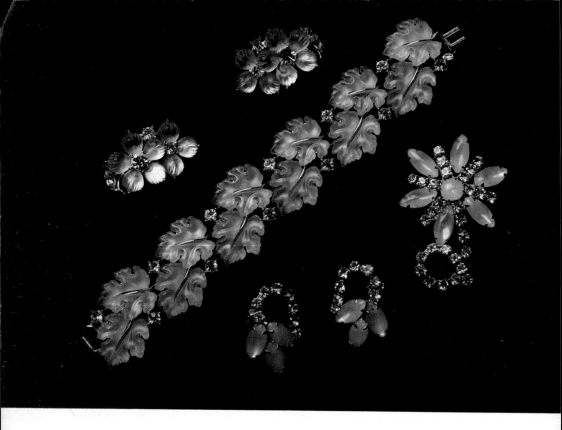

Lemon-up
Signed Listner earrings showing glass petals and rhinestones at center. Exceptionally well done, c. 1950's-$25. Moonstone type caboshons with yellow rhinestones. Tremendous reflection—$65. Signed Listner lemon colored glass leaf bracelet with yellow rhinestones, c. 1960's—$45.

It should be noted that the prices that appear in this book are those established by the many dealers whose pieces were used to help depict costume jewelry. The prices therefore tend to be regional dealing basically with the eastern seaboard. As yet, this author feels prices are nominal for many pieces and with the market ever increasing and less merchandise available, prices will begin to spiral upward.

Being linked arm-in-arm with the fashion industry, one notices that from time to time trends do overlap and are seen in repetion. Establishing a ten-year time line for styling is helpful, but can only be used as a flexible guide to help identify some jewelry styles. *All That Glitters*, attempts to give the reader a pleasant romp through the world of costume jewelry. By reviewing the social, political and economic changes America dealth with during the last 60 years, the reader will be better prepared to place costume jewelry in its proper era and begin to understand

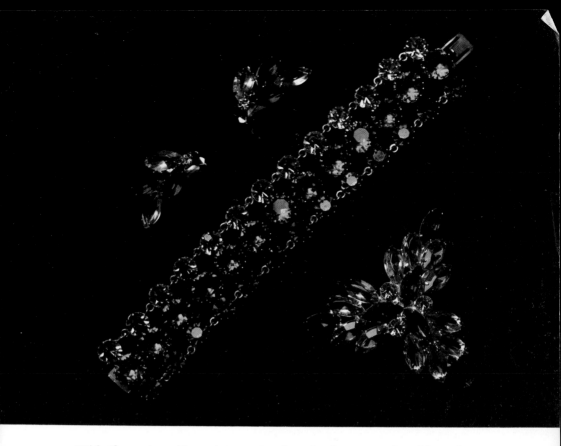

Wide three-strand bracelet ranging in color from purple to blues. Large brilliant stones, all prong set—$65. Earrings and pin set in turquoise and purple stones, c. 1940's—$25.

the whys and wherefores of the industry. It will become apparent that the leaders of the costume crusade held the pulse of the American woman; it catered to her wants and changing needs throughout the last 60 years. Although styles and forms changed frequently, one constant remained and allowed the industry to prosper through the years. From the very beginning the costume jewelry industry was bent on the idea that it could produce quality and quantity at an affordable price for every woman. Just looking in Mom's old jewelry box will witness their success!

In the past, this jewely has been called junk, fashion or costume; today it has a new name, collectible. The junk that Nana kept in a shoe box for the kids to play with is now being searched out at flea markets and antique stores by those same kids.

Above all, costume jewelry is fun and flash. It makes the statement, "Look at me." It evokes thoughts of bright lights, good times and a sense of self esteem. It is "All That Glitters."

*The sparkle of colored stones is evident in this selection of pins. Various designs in cut, color and clarity show the individual qualities of each of these pieces. Together they are a true representation of **Glitter** at its best.*

Part 1
Jewelry Histrionics

Costume jewelry may have graced the world in the 1920s but the forms in use go back to ancient times. Each society from the beginning of mankind used jewelry. Whether it be beads, shells, frit (early glass), animal vertibrae or rhinestones, each decoration was merely a reflection of the times in which it was adorned. Archaeologists and anthropologists beam from ear to ear when jewelry is found on an excavation sight. These finds give the social scientists tremendous insight into the workings of a society. The materials used, the metal work done, the decorative forms taken, all aid in understanding the spirit of the times.

Why jewelry at all? This is an interesting question and can only add to the understanding of why the world accepted costume jewelry in the 1920s. Jewelry in the past was not always used for pure decoration and ornamentation. Dating back to primitive man and up through the Renaissance, some jewelry forms were used to ward off evil and death as well as to show strength and achievement. By the Renaissance, jewelry was even being used as weapons; witness compartment rings for holding poisons! As societies developed jewelry began to denote social status, wealth and often held religious and political significance.

As the world grew, form became more developed. Once gold was found during the Bronze Age, the stage was set. By the time of the Greeks and Romans, the use of gemstones was entrenched along with the new use of color. Precious stones used today were virtually all being put to use in Rome.

One of the most popular forms of jewelry in ancient times was the ring. Egypt made the ring popular, inventing the modern day signet ring and the so-called poison rings which have been unearthed in mummies tombs. The Roman civilization further popularized the ring by using it not only as a status symbol but by instituting the tradition of the ring used to show betrothal.[1]. By the time of the Middle Ages, rings had attained both political and religious significance. It was under Charlemagne that laws were passed that allowed only laiety who were nobles or royalty to wear jewelry. Hence much of the jewelry of the times was made for the clergy. Entering into the 18th and 19th centuries the use of diamonds in rings made them an even more desirable property. With fashions of the late 19th century using gloves to complete the evening attire, rings lost some ground. However, by the 1920s, and the loss of the gloved hand, once again rings came to the fore.

Earrings were another popular jewelry form brought down from ancient times. For all the mothers who have worried about their sons wearing earrings, take heart. This form has a definite masculine as well as feminine history. Perhaps transplanted from Asia, when earrings first appeared in Egypt they were an

Collection of clear rhinestone earrings, both hanging and in spray form, c. 1940's-1950's. $25 each pair.

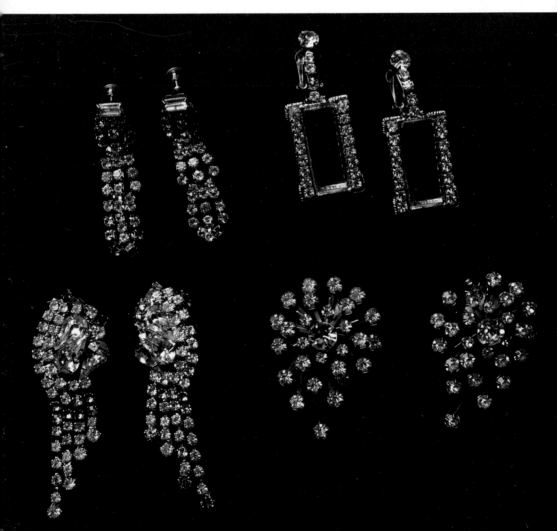

overnight success. Large pendant earrings as well as studs were seen.

The Etruscans have been credited with the hoop earring and by the time of the Greeks, earrings had evolved into four basic types. In Greece the fashion of the day was not only the stud and the pendant but also the boat shaped and spiral shaped earring.[2] The Romans later added the ball and the chandelier type earring. In Europe such notables as Shakespeare and Sir Walter Raleigh also donned the earring.[3] By the 17th century, both men and women were adorned with earrings.

With the advent of Charles I the style lost favour and the only men who still wore ear-rings were pirates and gypsies.[4] The 18th century saw new technology and earrings became bigger and bolder and at times longer. The 19th century brought continued success but late in the 19th century the fashion industry turned to hair pieces and adornment which overshadowed the earring. In the February 4, 1920, issue of the *Jewelers Circular*, earrings are mentioned as coming back after several years absence. Throughout the entire 20th century, earrings came on very strong and became one of the most creative forms in the costume jewelry world.

Bracelets too have a long history. The Egyptians wore bangles and even hinged bracelets of gold and glass. Seen also at this time were arm bracelets. The Romans made popular the upper arm bracelet that would become increasingly popular after World

Fifteen plastic bangles, many molded, some hand carved, a favorite in the 30's and the more the merrier. Colors ranged from blacks to reds and oranges to greens. Value $15-$20 each.

Far East influence from '20s to '40s. Red niello bracelet marked sterling designs show figural gods, c. 1940. Value $25. Large filigree bracelet with barrel clasp, c. 1920s. Value $65. Black and silver niello bracelet signed sterling and Siam, c. 1940s. Value $25. Green scarab glass drop earrings with screw backs, c. 1920s. Value $35. Scarab ring with real scarab hand set in mount. Setting marked sterling, 1920s. Value $35.

War I when sleeves became shorter or non-existent due to the shortage of dress material. With the coming of the Middle Ages, bracelets lost favour and remained a stepchild of the jewelry world well into the 19th century due to the fashion dictate of long sleeves. By the 20th century bracelets both arm and wrist came into vogue with the shift in fashion from long to short sleeves. One of the most popular bracelet forms to come along in the 1920s was that of the bangle which can be harkened back to the iron "slave-bracelets" of the Roman Empire. The trend in design to shorter or no sleeves had great repercussions all the way to the Papacy as seen by an article presented in the *New York Times*, February 3, 1922 whereby the display of shoulders and arms was frowned upon by the Pope. This prompted a circular to diplomats of the Holy See asking them that at official receptions where clergy would be present, a note accompany invitations informing women to dress in a less décolleté manner. Bare arms may have shocked the Pope but it opened the door for the bracelet to thrive.

Burial ground excavations back to pre-historic times gives evidence that the necklace was one of the earliest forms of decoration known to man. Stated by J. Anderson Black in his book, *The Story of Jewelry*, "Perhaps the earliest pieces so far discovered were three fish vertebrae necklaces found in a grave near Monaco...[5] The necklace has enjoyed great popularity throughout the ages. The knowledge of the Egyptians and King Tuts tomb attests to the beauty of the necklace even then and would be copied in bib necklaces in the late twenties and thirties and reached their height in the fifties as costume jewelry came into its own. The Egyptians also brought the collar and the choker into popularity seen then in the form of beads.

The necklaces of the Greeks were also in bead form composed of glass, gold and stone. The Greeks also began to use chain around the neck. Here one sees the employment of pendants and medallions in geometric forms. The Romans continued to carry out the chain effect with stones. By the Renaissance the gold chain was here to stay both light and heavy weight for both sexes. Jewelled chains were also popular at the time. By the 17th century with new knowledge of setting stones, necklaces were fully entrenched in the fashion world and would enjoy supremacy in the jewelry world well into the 20th century. Coming out of the Victorian age into the early 20th century, necklaces were stiff and morbid with jet being the mainstay around a lady's neck. A combination of influences from Europe, Russia, Egypt and the Orient along with the trend to imitate diamonds would bring the necklace into the fore as a glittering showpiece in the costume jewelry world.

Three-tier bib type choker necklace. Value $35. Accompanied by prong set earrings. Value $15-$20. Circa 1940.

Brushed gold became popular in the fifties and sixties. Signed Coro, brushed gold with pearl centers—$25. Signed BSK circle pin—$15. Mum pin done in brushed gold—$15.

History also tells us of the modern day brooch. Although found in Rome, the brooch was not popular as a decoration until the Middle Ages where it was worn in a circular form in Western Europe. Due to the dress code of the Renaissance the brooch took on new importance as ornamentation for both men and woman displayed at the shoulder, waist, neck and on hats. Throughout the 17th and 18th century the brooch continued to gain favor all throughout Europe and by the 19th century more color and imagination went into the creation of this decoration. By the 1920s the brooch, although not number one in the jewelry hit parade, began experimenting in form from small to large, from single to twin brooches and to pendulums and drops. As the years went on the brooch would become a mainstay in 20th century fashion becoming more and more elaborate and defined. It is in the form of art deco that the brooch radiates in the costume jewelry field.

Before turning our attention to the costume jewelry world fully, hair ornaments should be discussed. It was seen throughout history in the realm of jewelry. By the time costume jewelry became entrenched as a style, many hair ornaments were passé. This was due to the bobbing of womens hair in the 1920s. The hair ornament for a time the mainstay in the jewelry world was being produced all throughout the twenties in fine gems but gained little or no favor in the transition to the costume jewelry world. In the early stages of the costume jewelry many of the companies were heavily involved in hair ornaments and trinkets, or what the industry called utility pieces, but quickly turned to other forms of jewelry once short hair was here to stay.

The world entered the twentieth century with a bang. The full understanding of the Industrial Revolution was just being digested, the country was looking for something new. The Victorian drab and overstuffed look was out. War brought us to a strong sense of self along with much advanced technology and the understanding that we were not alone but could be influenced by styles and cultures across the seas. Women began to look at themselves as individuals, as not only mothers and wives but as a working force.

The stage had been set in the 20 short years from the birth of this century. The world would never be the same, speed, youth, technology and ingenuity would take over. The costume jewelry industry sensing the change and the new roles that society was moving toward would soon throw out the hair clips and pins. The industry would then break past tradition that only "good" jewelry should be worn and embark on a journey to give everyone the ability to adorn baubles, bangles and beads!

Signed Listner pin with blue and turquoise stones on brushed gold—$65. Emerald cut pin with clear rhinestones—$40.

17

1920's Buckles—including Marcasite and cut steel buckles with black leather backings. Value $20. Cut steel shoe buckles signed "Frank Brothers" showing silveroid setting and pasted stones. Value $25. Cut steel and marcasite buckles. Value $15.

Part 2
Trends and Influences
1920-70

1920s

The term roaring is appropriately given to the 1920s for it was a decade of swift change; politically, economically and socially, that would redesign the face of our nation forever. The 20s was a coming of age for America and can be seen through all facets of life.

Emerging from World War I, the nation was on a high and our self esteem was mounting. We had proven that we could protect ourselves and had emerged from conflict as a strong world leader. The 20s were a time of rejoicing and showing off. It was to be, according to President Harding, a return to "Normalcy". A time for flash, to honor heroes, to envision that bigger was better, a time of daring and changing morality. Costume jewelry fit right into the spirit of the times, it was glitz, glamour and glitter. Life was, in essence, a bowl of cherries.

Harding's "Normalcy" was a bit premature, for the atmosphere in the 20s was one of change with a capital "C". In August of 1920 women in America were given the right to vote. Prohibition was in but liquor was flowing and a new establishment, the "speak-easy," was born. Women were even smoking. In a report of the *Jewelers Circular* of February 1, 1922, there is mention of a market for "smoking things for womanfolk".

The beginnings of a strong middle class were evolving in the 1920s. Small independent businesses sprang up all over. With Henry Ford leading the way, the work day was lessened to eight hours, giving leisure time and its activities a new meaning. Movies and music began to take a stronger hold on America, while the radio was now king, bringing news and entertainment into every home. Three of the largest industries in the twenties were automobile, radio and films. By 1926 nearly 100 million people a week were going to the movies! The use of the automobile was becoming common place and by the end of the 20s there were nearly 5 million cars in production.[1]

Marcasite and sterling—Ribbon design bracelet marked sterling, c. 1920s. Value $50. Pair of marcasite monogram pins on sterling popular at the turn of the century and thru the 1920s. This fashion was revived in the 50s with rhinestones. Round pin value $85. Oblong pin value $45.

Entering the 1920s, jewelry was tightly following the trends of the dress designers of Europe and the fashion industry as a whole. Fashion, during this time, was in the throes of a dilemma. The first two years of the 1920s saw hemlines up, down and up again. Necklines and waists following suite. By 1921, the length of the gown was a hot issue in the news. In January of that year the American Dress League held an exhibit of gowns hoping that the American women would conform to what they felt was desirable. The mode of dress consisted of a satin blouse, knickerbockers and a drape like covering with snaps at the shoulder and waist. The reason for this so called "Knickerbocker" gown was given by exhibit speaker Mrs. Owen Kildare, "It will reduce the cost of living and we will eliminate a great deal of crime, for which they say the immodest dresses are responsible."[2] In the February 16, 1921 issue of the *New York Times,* it was reported that the Philadelphia clergy was trying to fix the measurement of a "moral" gown. In outrage Dr. Elizabeth Sloane Chesser was quoted as saying, "I never heard of anything so ridiculous. If these old gentlemen were psychoanalized it might be found that their excessive interest in women's dress had a significance at which they would be surprised. I think the dress of today is good

Far East influence is shown with bib necklace with silver and turquoise beads, c. 1920s. Value $65. Necklace and bracelet set 1000 silver marked on barrel clasp of necklace and cyclinder clasp of matching bracelet. Good workmanship shown in filigree work, c. 1920s. Value $150 for set.

and healthy. I hope long dresses will never again be brought in. This is the age of youth and everyone ought to remember it.[3] By late February, the *New York Times* of the 21st was reporting that the knee length and higher skirts were doomed, long waists were in and bright colors were out. By 1923 the clamour of popular demand overruled the fashion industry and sport dresses, shorter dresses and bright colors were the fashion.

Styles of the twenties dictated to the jewelry industry. The waistlines would decide the length of the necklaces, the sleeve length determined the amount of bracelets in vogue. When waistlines were long, necklaces followed suite in beads and ropes. Throughout the 20s the necklace remained a prominent piece of jewelry. Due to the shortage of material after the war, dress styles featured short-sleeves for day-wear and no sleeves for evening. This gave rise to the use of arm bracelets as well as wrist bracelets. By 1921 the bangle was back, and the rope was making a strong bid. By 1924, the flexilbe bracelet was here to stay. Many of these bracelets took their lead from a Russian inspiration that swept the fashion world in the first half of the 1920s.

The trend away from the wearing of gloves allowed the ring to resurface as a prominent accessory. By 1924 rings were large and

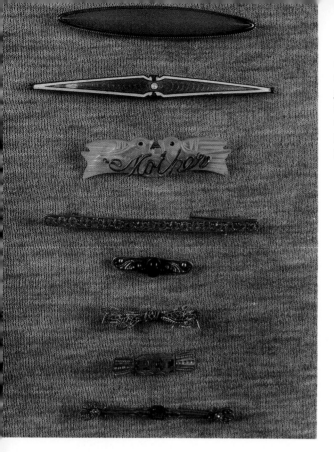

Bar Pins—Seen from 1900 into 1930s, collection ranges from amber on sterling, mother of pearl, amethyst on sterling, bow pins, name pins, and rhinestone bar pins. Value $5-$35.

by 1925 they were sporting twin stones. In hair fashion the bobbing of womens hair not only caused a moral upheaval but brought the earring back into fashion. Previously earrings were of the button type. Once hair was short, long earrings became the style of the day. By 1925 earrings were glittering, long and narrow.

Bar pins, lockets and brooches were also being seen in the costume jewelry world. The brooch was evolving in three styles, single stones, pendants and cluster brooches. The locket would remain a strong keepsake and reappear in the forties with even greater popularity. Bar pins were a Victorian hold over but were taking on new forms of ovals and rounds.

Due to new cultural awareness from across the seas, jewelry took on Russian, Egyptian and Oriental motifs. The old forms were also being challenged with the advent of the tassel, the dropped pendant and hanging garlands. The door to the world was opened and the jewelry and fashion industry were quick to incorporate it into their styles. During this time fashion designers such as Eisenberg in the United States and Co-Co Chanel of France were designing costume jewelry for their new dress designs and boosted the costume jewelry industry to greater heights. By 1923 ancient forms were being combined with not only old Victorian standbys but even American Indian designs. By 1925 the trends turned to the Persian look with bib and collar necklaces coming to the fore along with elongated earrings and flexible brooches. Lines were becoming softer, sportswear for women was more in evidence and there was a growing acceptance of the three piece set, (earrings, necklace and brooch). New technology was also entering the picture by the middle of the 20s. The mounts for jewelry were less and less evident as part of the jewelry design. Clusters of stones or pavé settings was becoming popular. No longer was the mount to be seen, but rather hidden by stones. The idea of open spaces was being incorporated in design work for the first time.

During the infancy of costume jewelry came the 1925 Internationale Des Arts Decoratifs in Paris. From this exposition would be born a new style of life, Art Deco. The theory was to turn to simple forms, modernistic designs, to incorporate nature into art and to view the designer as an artist. Lines should be clean, color should be defined and the ancient design modified and modernized. The art deco movement had far reaching appeal in furniture, architecture, literature, arts and crafts and by the 1930's it was firmly entrenched in the world of costume jewelry. As early as 1926 jewelry would be referred to as "painting in gems."[4] All new ideas of strict contours, three dimension and geometric

Bakelite bangle bracelets, early form of decorative plastic, c. 1930s. Value $15 each.

Citron colored faceted crystal beads with clear crystal rondeles. This piece demonstrates early clasp, c. 1920s. Value $25-$30. Amber color bohemian glass beads with crystals 18" long beads faceted and graduated in size. Turn of the century piece. Value $45.

designs were being innovated in the jewelry field. Fringes began to be used on short necklaces and earrings. The brooch often took the form of triangles or pyramids. The art deco period also can take credit for introducing another media to the jewelry world, that of plastic. Although invented by Leo Hendrick Baekaland in 1909, by the late 20s and well into the thirties, bakelite jewelry was worn in the forms of bracelets, earrings, necklaces and brooches.

Costume jewelry, still in its childhood in the 20s, was clinging to the old. It had not yet been fully accepted so often one would find rhinestones or colored stones set in eighteen karat white gold to imitate the platinum found in precious jewelry settings. Pearls were still popular and would remain as a standby throughout the jewelry world right up through the present.

Because of the gaiety and brightness of the twenties, crystals and rhinestones imported from Austria became more and more popular. By the late 20's store catalogues held pages and pages of the new costume look. Imitation jet took its turn at the helm in costume jewelry, taking its lead from the popularity of real jet necklaces during the Victorian Era. Colored amber beads also held favor in the twenties, again reaffirming the Victorian era. The times reached back once again to the past and brought forward marcasite. This mineral, not stone, became popular because of its shining nature. It had been used since the 17th century to imitate the diamond. By the end of the 1920s synthetic stones which resembled rubies, emeralds, diamonds and birthstones were all being worn. Due to a fascination with Africa and the Orient, Ivory became a favorite in the 20s and with rising costs, vegetable ivory extracted from nuts, was being used for small beads. Of all stones and beads that would fall in and out of favor throughout the history of costume jewelry the Rhinestone would be seen as a constant theme to last decade after decade in the industry. The subject of rhinestones will be dealt with in a later chapter but suffice it to say that once Co-Co Chanel used rhinestones to illuminate, accentuate and excite her fashions there was no turning back. Today one can't honestly say the words costume jewelry without seeing an image of rhinestones.

1930s

By the end of the 1920s America was humming, trade was booming, jobs were plentiful, wages were high. Fashion and jewelry reflected the image of a fat cat. On October 29, 1929 the roaring and the glittering of the 20s came to a swift halt. The stock market had collapsed and the country was thrown into financial turmoil. The nation was thrown back on its heels, everything stopped, unemployment was rampant, putting food on the table became a priority, something no longer taken for granted. The thought of buying a new dress was comical, but the costume jewelry industry would flourish. A new dress may have been out of the question, but a cheap piece of jewelry to enhance

1930's large pin with multi-faceted prong set red stones. Value $45.

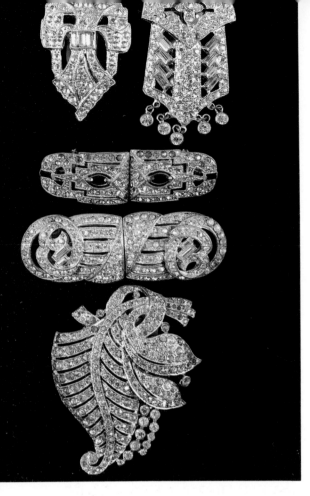

Rhinestone Clips—Signed "Nile" clip with silver backing, c. 1930s. Value $10. Deco influenced clip with silver backing, c. 1930. Value $10. Pin and pair of clips combination featuring pasted rhinestones with black stones in center, c. 1930s. Value $20. Rhinestone clips, same as above. Clip signed "Trifari" in leaf pattern, c. 1930s. Value $25.

an old dress was affordable and desirable to help put some glow into a depressed situation. On January 30, 1931 an ad appeared in the *New York Times* for Gimbles stating they had available 5000 earrings, necklaces and brooches of costume jewelry ranging from .79 to $2.79 at the lowest prices in the city. If costume jewelry was on a trial basis in the twenties, the economic situation of the early thirties made it acceptable as a household word.

If the 20s could be characterized as glitter and glitz, the 30s can be called classy, sleek and glamorous. In fashion the styles were trim and sleek; a silhouette effect. Following the art deco traditions, lines were simple and direct. Hemlines were constantly changing, square pads were added to shoulders and backs were plunging for evening ware. If the moral question of dress in the twenties was the length of a skirt, the question in the thirties was the slack. Clothes in general had become non confining to go with the times. The straight lines only enhanced the need and acted as a showcase for costume jewelry.

Pearl and rhinestone collar. Value $35. Silver pin signed "Ora" featuring rhinestones and marcasites, c. 1930. Value $15.

"Co-Co Chanel" Flamingo—base metal with rhinestones. Piece in need of repair, c. 1920-1930. Value $75.

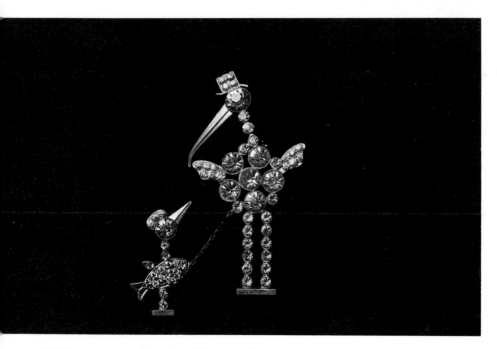

1930's stork novelty pin with pasted stones—$45.

The mood of the country was almost that of escape. The early years had devastated many and the movies and the big bands became a Mecca for fantasy. The times saw the birth of Las Vegas, and the airplane streaking across the skies making time almost stand still. When Marlena Dietrich and her compatriots walked across the screen in slacks a new fashion was here to stay. Interest was now shown in the lives of the rich and famous who were slowly replacing the 20s heroes of sports and war. Hollywood began to dictate style and the stars became the talk of the thirties. Hollywood fashion became so important that by 1931, Samuel Goldwyn brought Co-Co Chanel to Hollywood to introduce styles through the screen and update his costume department.[5] Also seen at this time in Hollywood was the work of William Hobé whose designs in costume jewelry for the stars captured America.

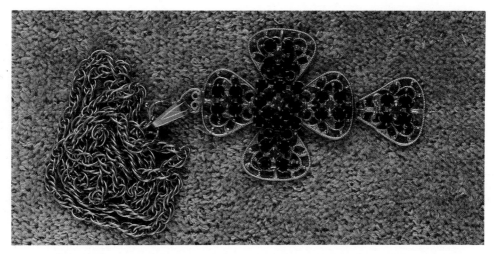

Signed "Hobé" cross with hand set garnet type stones, gold filled 30s-40s. Piece shows beautiful detail and intricate filigree work. Value $100-$200.

Throughout the decade, costume jewelry was on the rise. The simple elongated look of dresses only enhanced the viability of costume jewelry. Large pieces influenced by Egypt and the 1920s discovery of King Tut's Tomb became prevalent. Hats were in and with them came the rhinestone hat clip and pin. Characterized by geometric design; bracelets, clips and necklaces were the rage in 1933. New medias were being experimented with including wood, tortoise shell and coral.

By the middle of the thirties the rhinestone was queen in costume jewelry. It was stated in the 1935-36 Sears Catalogue, that

Hat Pins—used from 1890-1930s, shown here pins range from carnival glass to scarabs, colored glass, art nouveau sterling, celluloid, coral, mother of pearl and glass.

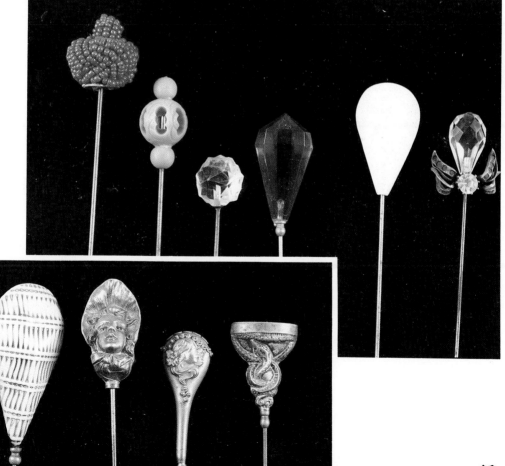

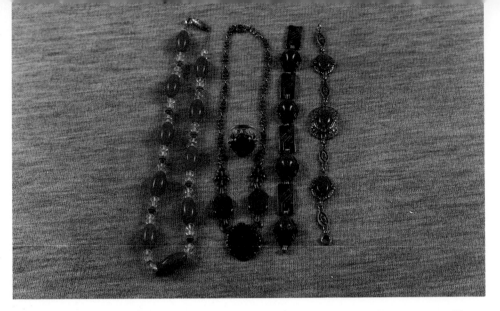

Carnelian—popular from the turn of the century, carnelians seen well into the 30s. L. to R., carnelian beads with crystal spacers on chain with barrel clasp, c. 1910. Value $45. Three stone necklace with marcasite hand set, c. 1920. Value $65. Carnelian and marcasite ring marked sterling, c. 1910-20. Value $55. Deco influenced bracelet with enamel links, c. late 1920s-30s. Value $45. Marcasite and carnelian bracelet marked sterling, c. 1920s. Value $35.

Five plastic pieces all from the 1930s including hinged bracelet, disc bracelets, bangles with silver plate, hand carved bangle and hand carved pin with no safety clasp. Value $10-$30.

Pizzazz!
Ring collar prong set with clear
rhinestones falling into graduated
lengths, c. 1930's—$95. Earrings
prong set clip-ons, c. 1930's—$25.

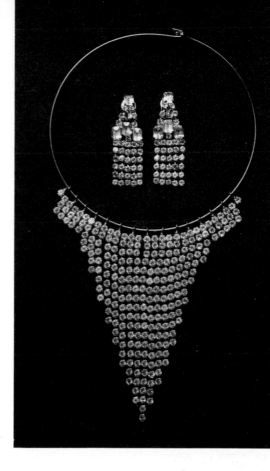

rhinestones were "most necessary, useful costume accessories for the fall and winter season."[6] It was now evident to the public that rhinestones were inexpensive enough to have different ones for every dress. If diamonds were forever, then rhinestones were for today and tomorrow one could buy more.

By the mid-thirties, not only was the pyramid and triangle popular in clips but the choker also came into vogue due to the influence on dress design of the Duchess of Windsor. By 1937, fall fashions were showing high waists and high necks taken from the Dutchesses wedding gown. The choker was used to enhance the high necks and whether studded with pearls or rhinestones this neckware found a place in the world of costume jewelry. Floral jewelry also came of age in the mid-thirties and was accepted immediately by the public along with novelty pieces of fruit and vegetables. Scottie dog pins, too, received favor due to F.D.R. and Eleanor. Colored stones such as amethyst and rose quartz were also popular at this time.

The thirties saw costume jewelry turn away from sterling and white gold and begin to use base metals, brass and by the end of the thirties rhodium which gave a visual effect of platinum. The use of gold in fine jewelry was on the rise so the costume jewelry industry took to gilding their product. The influence of Russia and the Orient continued and colored stones grew more and more popular. Materials used in the thirties were rhinestones, maracites, onyx, chrysoprase, carnelian, rose quartz and amethyst.

The Worlds Fair of 1939 promised progress and a bright future filled with new technical advances. We had come out of the depression on our feet and the world looked rosy for the future, but amid all the hope and bright spirit there was a hint of tension. . . war.

The costume jewelry industry was quick to pick up on this theme as can be seen from an article published in the *New York Times* on March 28, 1939. In essence a proposal was under consideration by the Bead, Stone and Glass Importers Assoc. to bring 5,000 Czechoslovakians to America to teach between 50,000 and 75,000 workers the secrets of bead and glass working for costume jewelry. At the time the government was about to classify all goods from Moravia, Bohemia and Slovakia as German and the U.S. wanted to boycott all goods from German dominated areas.

The acceptance and strength of costume jewelry can be further seen when Mrs. Theodore Roosevelt Jr., in October of 1939 sponsored a jewelry bazaar of large costume pieces with Oriental motif to raise funds for Chinese War Orphans. Sold at the bazaar, it was reported, were 4000 pieces for a total of $1,000.[7]

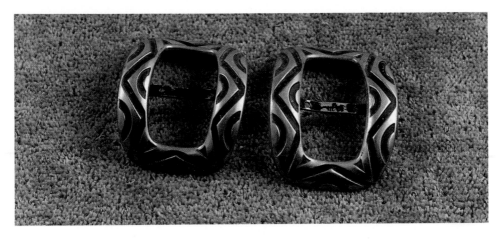

Pair of shoe buckles marked France demonstrating the Deco influence, c. 1930-40s. Value $40.

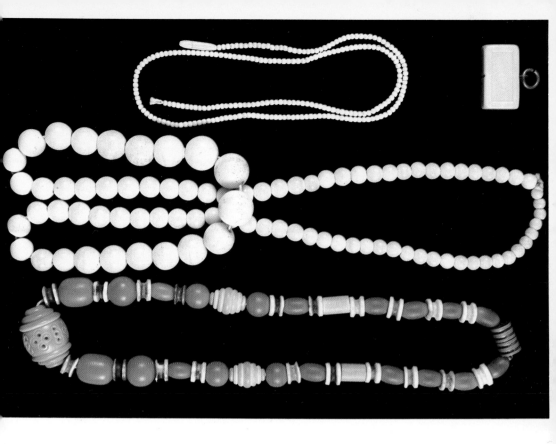

Ivory—Miniature strand of ivory with ivory barrel clasp. Turn of the century. Value $30. French Ivory pin advertising Proctor and Gambel Ivory Soap, c. 1940s. Value $25. Bone graduated beads on rope. Value $25. Vegetable Ivory necklace showing graduated beads with hand carved central beads in shades of peach, tan and beige. Barrel clasp in brass. Value $35.

1940s

By 1941 came the bombing of Pearl Harbour and Americans found themselves once again in a World War which they felt could never happen after the "Big One". The impact of World War II may have very well changed the course of America. Certainly the economic and social attitudes of the country were forced to change. Although women had received the right to vote in 1920, by 1941 they were not only voting but working in full force. A new sense of individualism and self confidence was emerging. With the men away at war much of their tasks were turned over to young adults and with that the so-called "teen-ager" was born. youth was "in" and would stay in as the look of America.

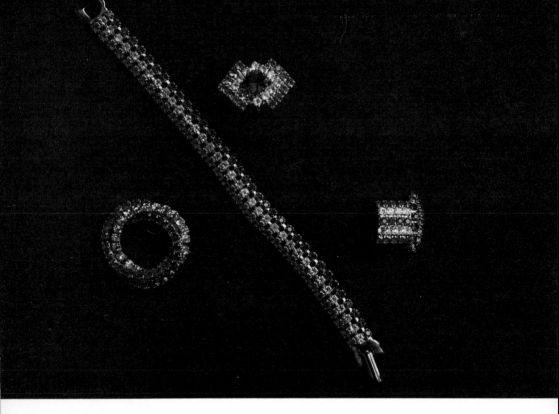

Patriotic
Red, white and blue rhinestones set in circle pin, ring, hat pin and
three-strand bracelet. Circle pin—$10, ring—$10, hat pin—$15,
bracelet—$25.

The fashion industry was quiet, slacks were the dress of the day with some 18 million women entering the working force. Costume jewelry on the other hand was growing. What had been born as a fad was now beginning its 15th year of true acceptance and an increase in sales had been seen over 1939. By 1940 costume jewelry was being sold for every mood. It was making statements as to the personality of its wearer. The industry, although soon to be hit with war-time restrictions had survived its birth and adolescence to enter maturity.

Because of the war, money was in plenty, but goods were scarce. By the mid 1940s women were spending 1 billion 3 million dollars on jewelry.[8] Even during the war the women wanted to feel and look glamorous. Costume or "junk" jewelry was a way to achieve the look. Once a copy cat of precious jewels costume jewelry now began to set design trends.

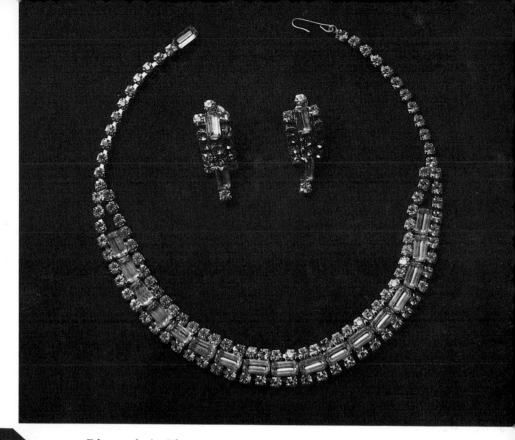

Rhapsody in Blues
Blue rhinestone collar type necklace. Value $65. Pair of blue rhinestone earrings, clip-on, in prong setting. Value $15.

Drop necklace exemplifying 40's look. Value $45. Blue rhinestone bracelet. Value $65.

The war was a two edged sword for the jewelry industry. On the one hand early in 1941 sales were increasing and prices were holding due to the new developments of American designs and American material since the European market was closed. Seen now were new plastics, moonstones and American made pearls. Plastics came in the form of bracelets, necklaces and pins and were mostly hand carved and light weight. By May of 1941 the *New York Times* reported on the 16th, that a patent for lucite had been given to Maximilian C. Meyer president of Joseph H. Meyer Brothers a costume Jewelry manufacturer in New York. If new materials were booming, the other side of the sword saw by the middle of 1941, a shortage in metals and rhinestones. The government was beginning to restrict the use of white metal which was 90% tin. The cost of rhinestones reported in the June 28th issue of the *New York Times* had gone from 8 cents to 65 cents a gross for small stones and from 8 to 55 cents for medium and large stones. Aside from stones and metal, the government was also rationing ammonia and other chemicals essential for the plating process of jewelry making. Many of the jewelry manufacturing companies turned to the war time efforts. They stopped producing jewelry and began to aid the government in the manufacturing of dog tags, bullet caps and tips for bomb shells.

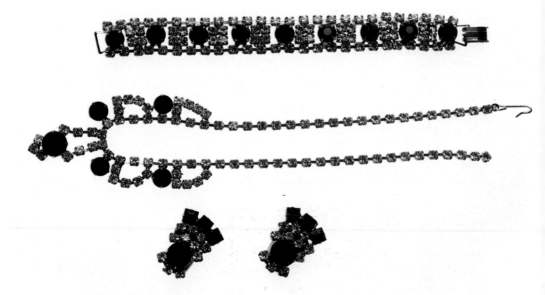

Bracelet and necklace featuring black glass beads prong set with rhinestones surrounding, clip-on earrings, c. 1940's. Value $95.

Never missing a step, the costume jewelry industry continued production turning to other forms of jewelry such as, spaghetti jewelry, a form of decoration where macaroni was used. They began to incorporate wood, glass, shells, nuts, seeds, and sterling into their designs. By May 31, 1942 the use of white metal, copper and rhodium had been curtailed. The industry quickly turned to sterling at a slightly greater cost. Sterling had more strength than white metal and one didn't need as much to create a piece of jewelry but it was harder to work with. In vogue came pearl inlays on silver and colored enameled wood. Small pins and insignias were the taste of the day along with lockets.

By 1943 Coro one of the leaders in costume jewelry was showing plastic with rhinestone but not just for day wear but for evening ensembles too. Ceramic pins came to the fore as did shell necklaces, leaf pins of acetate, leather leaf pins and glass flowers.

By the Spring of 1944 flowers had taken over the costume jewelry world. Flowers done in sprays of glass, plastic and ceremics used in pin, necklace and clip form were abundant. Hearts, too, were making a big splash. New on the fashion scene were heart pendants with lucite arrows that were worn on the shoulder.

Early plastics dating late 20s, 30s, and 40s, from top down; coral color molded orange chrysanthemum. Value $20. Stretch bracelet with pressed floral design originally sold with matching pin. Value $30. Pin in the form of a hat. Value $15. 1920s plastic pin with celluloid type backing surrounded with amber color rhinestones. Value $20. Belt buckle with metal backs, c. 1940s. Value $20. Molded plastic necklace in floral motif. Value $35.

The forties were epitomized by small pins, clips for sweaters, clip on earrings, plastic bracelets, and spray pins and sunbursts. By the end of the war, sanctions were still felt by the industry. Metals and stones were still hard to get. The craze for big returned and chunky jewelry became the look of the day. Simulated pearls combined with rhinestones returned stronger than ever and enhanced a regal look that would continue on into the 50s.

White glass popular in the 30s and again even bigger in the 50s. Necklace features white stones hand set showing gold color backing, c. 1930s—$25. Wrap-around white glass beaded bracelet, c. late 30s—$15. Drop clip-on earrings in red, white and blue hand set stones, c. 1940s— $25. Earring and bracelet set featuring white glass stones and rhinestones, earrings are clip-on and bracelet has safety chain, c. 1950s—$45.

By 1947, wholesale prices in the industry were down 25% but goods and metals were still scarce. Some predicted that better costume jewelry would continue to be set in silver even after metal restrictions were lifted. By the fall of 1947 the costume jewelry companies that had weathered the war years were looking for a big season. Coro stated in the *New York Times*, "pre-war prices and pre-war quality,"[9] and advertised they would be showing 5,000 different designs in necklaces, earrings, pins, bracelets and brooches. By the late 40s the industry began to see new trends toward femininity, the use of the pearl was in and a return to the antique forms of European paste jewelry became evident. The best bets for the 1947 season were earrings, necklaces and, close behind, small pins, with the essential materials in use being that of pearls and rhinestones.

The 1948 market was entered with gusto, sales were up by some 50% with the choker seen as a favorite over multi-stranded necklaces. Flowers were again seen as a constant motif in opaque whites, roses and blues. And fashion shows were incorporating diamonds and "junk" at the same time. Costume jewelry now was a big business fully entrenched in society.

Conflicting reports of losses and gains emanate from the 1949 season but the trend in costume was very strong and heading towards the sale of more expensive pieces. The pearl being a favorite for some years was faced with a rival in the introduction of Chalk beads. The line consisted of opaque white beads used in shapes of popcorn (bumpy beads), nuggets, globes and seed beads. Such noted firms as Coro, Trifari, Castlecliff, Rosenstein and D. Lisner all experimented with this line. White was definitely in for the summer of 1949. D. Lisner even went as far as naming their new line "White Magic."[10] Companies like Trifari were showing white enamel-like daisies, dog collars of pearls, chokers and plastics in soft hues of lavender, wedgwood and yellow.

The floodgates had been opened for the industry in 1949 and the rush of jewels flowed all the way to the college campuses. Here young ladies were boasting single strand necklaces worn 3 or more at a time and many bracelets. Hattie Carnegie features

Popular throughout the 1950s, this three piece white set was designed at Trifari in 1957. Value $25.

Sterling figural deer pin of Mexican origin demonstrating the Deco influence. By late forties and fifties Mexican jewelry was strong in the marketplace, c. 1940s. Value $25.

turquoise and ruby circlets with an oriental flare. Big, too, is returning in the form of oversized simulated pearls, jade and coral beads. One begins to see trends of the fifties establishing themselves in Mexican import jewelry and gold wash.

If production reports were mixed in the beginning of 1949, by the end of the year sales were up and the industry was booming. Trifari reported that buying was brisk and better lines were selling well. Coro was doubling their work staff and would employ some 2,000 workers. In a brochure entitled "Operation Profit" put out by Coro, it stated, "since 1938 total sales of costume jewelry have increased at a faster rate than total store figures, with higher cumulative mark-on than most major departments.[11]

1950s and 1960s

The 50s were a direct reaction to the worries, fears and stoicism of the 1940s. By the beginning of the decade America saw a softening of design, once again a clamour for bigger and better. The idea of a youthful America continued to flourish and young adults felt a new freedom as modern "teen-agers". Rock and roll was replacing the big band, souped up cars were replacing Dad's sedan. The push was on to get away from the cities and find a quieter way of life in the suburbs. If radio was the ears of the world in the 20s and 30s the birth of T.V. would become the eyes of the world by the 50s.

If Co-Co Chanel may have been the watchword in fashion in the late 20s and 30s, by the 50s, the name on everyones lips was Christian Dior. He brought with him to America a return to femininity and a softness in dress that had been lost for two decades. No respectable closet would be found without a rustling crinoline hanging in it. The March 31st issue of the *New York Times* told of a contract signed by Christian Dior with the Kramer Jewelry Co. to design costume jewelry. It was stated in the article that Mr. Dior would present 125 pieces of costume twice a year. Between dress and jewels, the Dior name was on every womans lips.

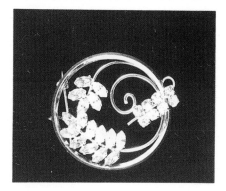

Signed "Dior" sterling pin and pendant featuring blue and clear rhinestones on circle pin, c. 1950s. Value $35.

If one had to sum up the look of 50s and early sixties in one word, it would be LARGE. The "bigger and better" syndrome was back. The chunkier and the clonkier the more appeal costume jewelry had. Women were making a statement. It was the time of the wide skirt and the wide jewelry. It was a time in costume jewelry of experimentation and freedom. It was a time when Guiliano Fratti of Milan would introduce cork beach jewelry dipped in gold and studded with rhinestones, when plastic fruit was not only seen on the table but on jewelry as well.

In style in the early 50s were whites, golds, pearls, rhinestones, coral and enamels. With the return of the black evening gown, rhinestones were now being featured as evening wear for the hair, neck and hand. Multiple bracelets were the thing and the "bigger the better."

By 1951 large chunky beads were being worn along side big pins with large square or cabochon stones in gold tone settings. Double end stick pins and rhinestone bar pins were also being featured. The end of 1951 saw the modern look establishing itself with the jewelry hit parade encompassing large stone pins, Heraldic jewelry, earrings and necklaces. Scatter pins were falling from grace.

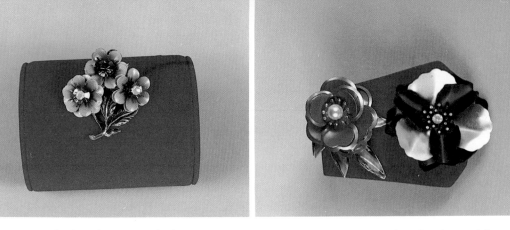

Enamel floral pin with large rhinestone centers, late 1950s. Value $15.

Two enamel floral pins with pearl centers, c. 1950s. Value $10 each.

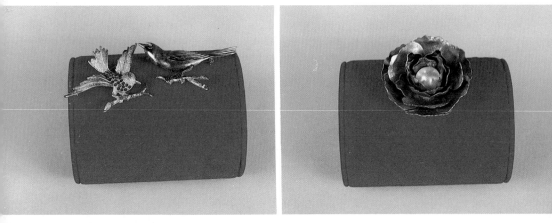

Two bird pins brushed gold and enamel featuring rhinestones, c. 1950s. Value $10 each.

Large floral brushed gold pin with pearl center. Value $15.

Jeweled bibs were the big news of 1952. This ancient form was now made up of pearls, rhinestones, jets and crystal for evening wear, in addition to gold medallions or gold beads or links. As for earrings the news was the hoop and the bigger the better. Teardrop and the button earring were also in vogue along with rhinestone branches. Arm bracelets in goldtone were being revived with fervor.

In 1953 the industry saw a shortage of rhinestones with the Czechoslovakian trade lines cut. Austria becomes the main source of good stones but even with increased production, the demand was too high to be met satisfactorily.

As America entered the mid-fifties, aluminum came on the scene in necklaces, bracelets, earrings and pins. The finish most

Bib necklace goldtone with red glass beads and matching earrings, c. 1950s. Value $45 set.

Goldtone necklace with pendant featuring coral type stone. Chain not original to piece. Pendant shows Greco-Roman influence with display of coins, c. 1950s. Value $35.

Signed "Coro" fleur de-lis locket popular in the 50s demonstrating both rhinestones and porcelain on a gold wash base. Value $15.

preferred was gold and the accessory most worn was the necklace. The most sought after necklaces at the time were made up of combinations of stones, metals and beads and took the forms of bibs, long chains, lavaliers and chokers.

Although the backbone of the industry was still the $1 item, the trend was shifting to more expensive costume jewelry.[12] By the end of the 50s, antique styles were returning and East Indian motifs were appearing on the scene. American tastes were heading toward native stones such as quartz, jade, opal and the return to classicism was being hinted at.

The 1960s were hectic years for America. They contained the hippie and the birth of the flower child. Materialism was out, nature was in. It was a time of great mourning with the assassination of a president and the leader of the civil rights movement. It was an era filled with protests, marches, sit-ins, lie downs. It was a period of great disillusionment with the questioning of Viet-Nam. It was Dr. Spock's America, the era of liberalism.

For the costume jewelry industry, it was the time of interpretation and creativity. Finer pieces were replacing the $1 and $2 pieces and a sense of sophistication enhanced the jewelry of the decade. Popularity rested in multi-strand necklaces, bibs, floral pins and drop earrings. Noted manufacturers were advertising in

1950s plastic jewelry, flowers the rage of the times. Value $10 to $15.

Prancing poodle pin very popular in the 1950s. This pin decorated with rhinestones, but many used pearls and fake diamonds. Saks-34th advertised poodle pins from $2.98 to $3.98 in the New York Times on November 4, 1951—$20.

Heart shaped rhinestone pin popular in the 1950s. Value $20.

1. Striking three-piece signed Sarah Coventry pin and clip-on earrings set in gold wash featuring large amber faceted prong set rhinestones, c. 1960—$25. 2. Signed Emmons clip-on silver earrings, c. 1950s—$15. 3. Signed Sarah Coventry floral pin with matching earrings displaying pearl centers, c. 1960s, $25 set.

Signed "Weiss" 3-piece moonstone and rhinestone set. Popular in the 1950s. Value $55.

Vogue Magazine with such slogans as "A splendid Splash, to wear with dash" by Trifari, "The Diamond Look" by Kramer and "Jewels of Legendary Splendor" by Hobé.

The trend in jewelry turned to the American Indian and turquoise. Although one of the oldest gemstones used, its largeness and brightness and the mood of America in the sixties brought it into favor. Often desired in years past for magical powers, by the sixties it was favored for its wonderous color.

Collection of Mexican sterling with abalone, c. 1950s. Value $25 each. Mexican silver bracelet with obsidian type stone, c. 1950. Value $35.

The most desirable color of turquoise being a bright blue, it can however be found in colors ranging from sky blue to green. It should be noted that the greener the piece, the less valuable it is. Mexico is known as the largest supplier of turquoise and in the United States good turquoise can be found in New Mexico, California, Colorado and Arizona. The best turquoise comes to the United States from Asia. Often combined with sterling or Mexican silver, turquoise appeared on the jewelry scene in the form of necklaces, earrings, belts, bracelets and rings.

By the 60s the costume jewelry industry was standing tall on its own feet and heading for even greater heights. Over a forty year period, they had proved themselves as legitimate. That which was to have been a fad, that which was to break with the custom of wearing only "good" jewelry, and that which was to have thrived on imitation proved an entity in its own right. An entity that would in its lifetime give pleasure to millions and become an innovator for modern designs in years to come.

American Indian—popular in late 1920s and 1930s seeing great resurgence in the 1960s. Pictured is silver beaded necklace with turquoise rosettes, c. 1920. Value $100. Thunderbird pin, unmarked with safety clasp, c. 1950. Value $15.

Pearl, crystal and rhinestone necklace with large hanging sphere. Rhinestones hand set, aurora borealis crystals set in a floral motif. C. 1950's-60's Value $45-$65.

Feather design stamped necklace with link chain. Representing the late 60s-70s influenced by King Tut gems. Value $50-$65.

Coral collection worn from Victorian times thru present. Branches represent pink Pacific coral, most precious form and found deep in the ocean—$60 and $40. 14k. pink coral ring, c. 1940, still being produced today—$150. Branch coral and bead necklace—$70. Red coral ring set in sterling—$40. Coral and marcasite earrings mounted on sterling—$40. Red coral branch necklace—$150.

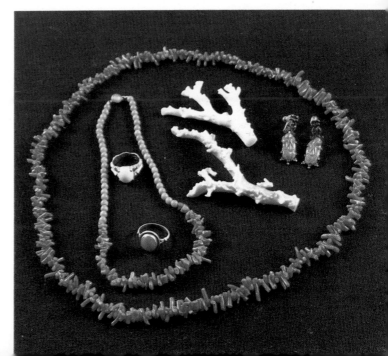

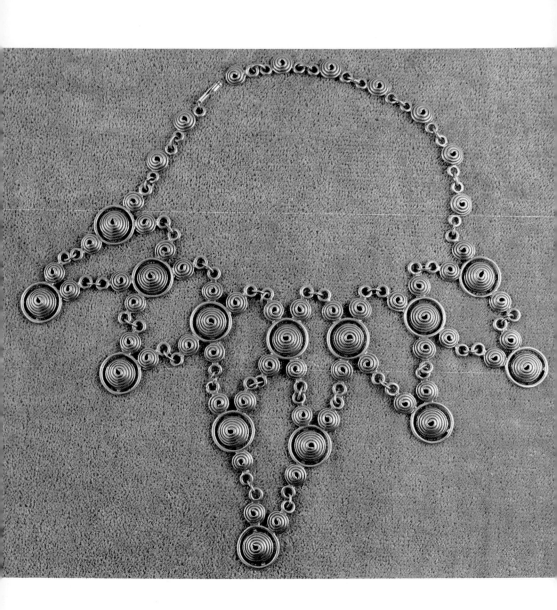

Large bib type necklace representing coil design showing both Deco and Egyptian influences. C. 1960-70 Value $45-$65.

Part 3
A Word About . . . . .

RHINESTONES

Perhaps no other material used signifies the costume jewelry world better than the rhinestone. Somehow when thinking about costume jewelry most people tend to see this shiny glass as a symbol of the industry.

In the past it has been called paste, stras, or brilliants and has a history of grandeur dating back thru the 17th, 18th and 19th century. Rhinestones are clear or colored glass that has been backed with a foil or a tin so that it may capture light and throw it back out, hence glitter. Gems such as diamonds have a reflecting ability whereas light would go right through the rhinestone without a foil backing. Paste and stras are quite synonymous with the paste being defined by M.D.S. Lewis in his wonderful book called Antique Paste Jewellery as "glass that has been cut into gemlike forms".

The history of glass can be traced back thousands of years and it was always considered valuable. By the Middle Ages, glass was much sought after and by the time of Queen Elizabeth I it became part of the royal dress. Whether it was valued for itself or later for its ability to imitate the gemstone look, glass, down through the ages, was an important commodity.

The Venetians took the lead in glass making perfecting the ability to produce a clear glass without impurities. But by the 17th century glass making moved to England. There, with a ban on the use of wood for stoking fires, and the use of coal as a replacement, came the invention of Flint glass which put England on the map as one of the leaders in glassmaking.

The stage had been set. New technology and tools were making glass ever more desirable. By the 18th century George Fredric Stras, a jeweler from Strasbourg, came to Paris and created a popularity for paste that would thrive into the 19th century. It was because of this man that paste began to be called Stras. At this

Sunburst Rhinestone pin with base metal backing rhinestones pasted, c. 1920s. Value $15. Newer sunburst dating 1950s multi-faceted rhinestones hand and paste set. Value $20. Oblong rhinestone brooch, c. 1930 (however displaying earlier design). Value $25. Rhinestone and simulated pearl necklace, c. 1940s-1950s. Value $45.

point in time paste was not in competition with diamonds but became its own entity. This would change however in the 19th century when rhinestones were used to imitate the diamond. The property of this material was much easier to shape and form than diamonds and much easier to cut. The designs effected were much more flowing and original than the stiffness of a diamond and soon became well accepted by the upper classes.

Pins of glitter—Top to bottom, first four pins demonstrate motif of the 1930s. Value $10-$15. Bottom pin signed "Phyliss" done in sterling with multi-faceted hand set stones in a leaf design, c. 1950. Value $45.

Clear rhinestones, l. to r. Rhinestone bracelet with major pear shaped stone, c. 1930s. Value $25. Super necklace with hand set multi-faceted emerald cut rhinestones, c. 1940s. Value $50. Rhinestone drop necklace with removable extension piece, c. 1940s. Value $40. Rhinestone bracelet displaying three large multi-faceted stones, c. 1930s. Value $25.

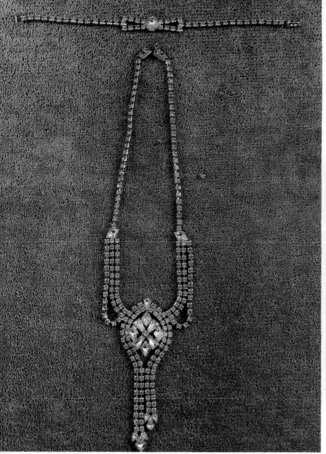

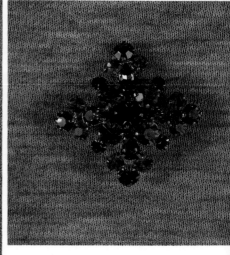

Magnificent Austrian rhinestone pin showing multi-colors of rose, green and lavender. Stones bright, showing good designs, c. 1930s. Value $25.

Bracelet and choker from the 1940s all handset rhinestones showing good workmanship and design. Value $25 and $50.

Rhinestone bracelet with imitation platinum setting, c. 1920s. Value $25. Signed "Trifari" brushed gold leaf earrings late 1940s. Value $10. Excellent hand set teardrops and oval pin, c. 1940s. Value $25. Late marcasite orchard pin marked West Germany, c. 1950s. Value $15.

Left:

Amethyst colored rhinestones—Signed "Sherman" bracelet showing pinks on silver with a black coating. Well cut rhinestones, hand set, c. late 1940s - early 50s. Value $55. Pins demonstrate hand set rhinestones on brushed gold, c. 1950s. Value $20 each.

Right:

Rhinestone bracelet in link pattern showing inset rhinestone centers, c. 1930s. Value $25. Pin featuring both clear and amethyst colored stones, c. 1930s. Value $25. Rhinestone pin with blue center stones, silver backed with safety clasp, c. 1930s. Value $25. Hand set rhinestone bow and arrow pin, c. 1950s. Value $20. Sterling bracelet with rhinestones pat. date 1925. Value $45.

*Clear rhinestone necklace and large spray pin with hand set rhinestones,
c. 1940-50s. Value $35 necklace, $20 pin.*

Signed "Emmons" goldtone spray pin with rhinestones. Value $20.

Signed "Weiss" pin displaying pear shaped Austrian rhinestones. Value $25.

Signed "Trifari" set. Brushed gold with green faceted stones, circa 1960s. Value $110.

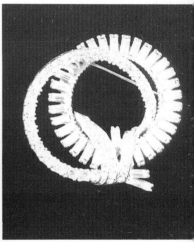

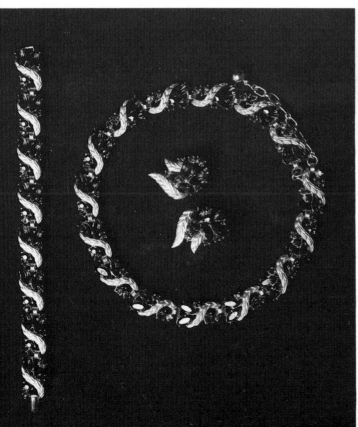

Signed "Ledo" circle pin on silver backing with safety clasp. Well designed with use of brilliant rhinestones hand set, c. 1940s-50s. Value $25.

Signed "Ora" cluster pin with hand set rhinestones, c. 1950. Value $12.
Signed "Emmons" sunburst brushed gold and rhinestones. Value $12.
Signed "Trifari" circle pin delicately done. Value $15.

"Hanover" watch set in a rhinestone pin with silver backing. Pin is double clasped, hand set and multi-faceted, c. 1950. Value $45.

Rhinestone necklace prong set rhinestones, c. 1920s. Value $45.

Small signed "Weiss" star piece with prong setting. Value $35. Larger signed "Weiss" brooch with prong set rhinestones and baroque pearl insets, masterful piece, c. 1950s. Value $95.

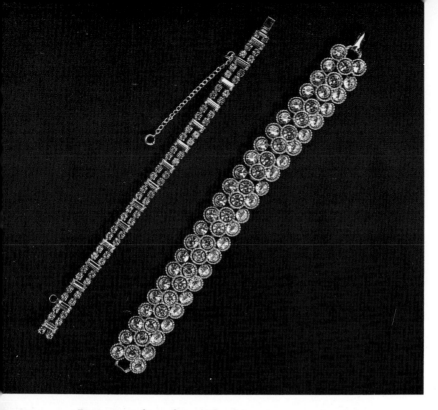

Prong set bracelet with rhinestones and safety
chain. Value $25. Listner bracelet of brushed gold
with rhinestones. Value $45.

Antique paste, now a very valuable commodity, can be
distinguished from the 20th century rhinestone quite easily. First
check the metal, remembering that modern rhinestones may have
sterling or gold settings, almost all of the antique past was set in
silver and late in the 18th and 19th century gold backs and gold
shanks appeared. Next look at the casting of early paste for one
can see sand marks depressed in the metal. On more modern
jewelry, the sand marks if present are raised, not depressed.
Another area to look at in trying to distinguish old paste from
new rhinestones are the way fittings are attached. Early paste had
the fittings attached to a piece of metal by hard soldering and then
the metal is attached to the jewelry by soft soldering. This method
prevented any damage to the glass which was soft in nature. Sizes
and shapes of stones also varied tremendously in the workmanship of the 18th century and the amount of different sized stones
in each setting was great. As time wore on shapes and sizing
became more uniform. By the 19th century, in order to imitate the
diamond, paste took the form of rounds or ovals. The foil to back
the rhinestones can also tell a tale, for early paste was backed by

copper and silver, newer stones backed by tin. When looking at the stones themselves, one can see a black spot in the center of the stone due to a paint that was applied to the settings on early pieces. This spot is absent on newer jewels.

All in all, antique paste has a regal look about it, the stones are a finer cut, the settings show more details and the pieces are lighter in weight than the modern rhinestone setting.

Entering the 20th century, rhinestones took their lead from the 19th century use as an imitator, and were considered junk or fake jewelry. It has not taken long for them to become an entity in and of themselves as the decades rolled on. They have, at this point in time, come full circle, as M.D.S. Lewis stated of antique paste, "At its best, it cannot be regarded simply as a mere simulation of something more valuable. It was not counterfeit Jewelry. . . Antique paste jewellery should be regarded as an art form in its own right."[1] Today with rhinestones of the 20s and thirties resurfacing and the new rhinestones of the 80s bureogning on the market perhaps the same is true!

Novelty grouping 1940-1960. Frog displays moveable parts. Animals all use rhinestones. Alligator pin in sterling. Value $15-$20.

MANUFACTURERS..

Headquarters for the costume jewelry industry in the United States is New York and Rhode Island although manufacturers can be found in more than 20 states. The industry as a whole grew by leaps and bounds in the late 20s and thirties with their products becoming more and more acceptable and desirable by the American woman. It is an industry of daring for it turned the tastes of America around 360 degrees as far as its acceptance of "fake" jewels. It weathered both poor image and war to arrive as one of the healthiest industries in America.

Books have been written with extensive lists of makers and marks and they certainly do that area justice. This section therefore will discuss only a few prominent makers whose names appear on their jewelry and can still be found at most flea markets and antique stores. Hot on the market today are names like Eisenberg, Hobé, Carnegie, Coro, Haskell and Trifari all putting out strong lines of costume with good quality stones and great design. The key to success for the industry was the ability to put out a well designed piece, consisting of good materials at an affordable price.

Eisenberg Jewelry a much sought after name in costume jewelry started out in business as a ready-to-wear clothing manufacturer. To add more eye appeal to the wear, Eisenberg began to put rhinestones, hand set in sterling on their fashions. At first they used no mark, but by the 1930s the pieces carried the mark Eisenberg then Eisenberg Originals and finally in 1950 pieces were marked "Eisenberg Ice". Stones used by Eisenberg were and still are some of the finest Austrian rhinestones around.

They are imported from the Swarovski Co. in the Tryrol region of Austria.[2] Eisenberg jewelry has a clarity and brightness that is matched by few.

"Eisenberg Ice"—signed pin featuring handset rhinestones. Workmanship and design outstanding as with brilliance of stones. Value $50.

Coro began its history back in 1902 under the name of Cohn and Rosenberger. It was a company with foresight as early on they saw the needs of the public and went about systematically supplying them. By the time of the depression they had already established a large factory in Providence, Rhode Island and from then on climbed a steady ladder to success. After World War II Coro was considered "numero uno" in the industry. The *New York Times* must have felt the same for there are constant references to Coro in articles concerning the costume jewelry industry.

Throughout its history Coro dealt under many trademarks with Corocraft being the top of their line. Credit for many fine designs coming from Coro must be given to designer Adolph Katz who, among other things; brought movable jewelry to the Company. Today Coro is easily found for they produced an abundance of goods. The Coro Plant now sits defunct at the entrance of Providence but its gifts to the costume jewelry world still live on.

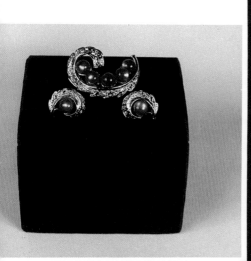

Signed "Coro" moonstone and rhinestone pin and earring set, c. 1950. Value $16 set.
Signed "Coro" necklace and matching pin, c. 1950. Value $45 set.

Earlier Coro pin hand set with brilliant rhinestones, c. 1940's. Value $15.

"Coro-Craft"—Pin and matching earring set featuring turquoise center stone, pearls and rhinestones set in paste with brushed gold finish, c. 1940s. Value $85.

By Coro: large pin of brushed gold with large prong set iridescent rhinestones. Value $35. Necklace of brushed gold links with tie design. Value $25.

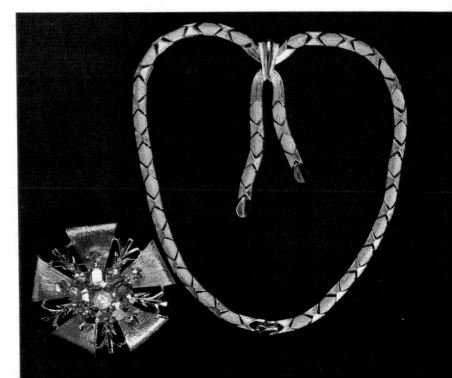

From left counter-clockwise, Signed "Coro" choker, signature on clasp. c. 1940s Value $45. Rhinestone hanging pin with prong set stones, c. 1940. Value $20. Pasted rhinestone pin with hanging teardrop, c. 1940s Value $20. Rhinestone mesh bracelet with unusual slide clasp. c. 1940s Value $25.

Necklace of gold links. Value $15. Earrings with gold open petals holding green and pink pastel stones. Value $10. Pearl center earrings with prong set pink rhinestones. Value $10.

65

Signed "Hobé" pieces, c. 1950s including bar pin of black beaded background with three red iridescent rhinestones—$25. Imitation turquoise stones mounted on gold circle pin with rhinestone frame—$35. Pair of petal earrings with green rhinestone centers—$25.

Signed "Hobé" earrings and three-strand necklace showing petal covered iridescent beads—$25.

When thinking of craftsmanship the name Hobé must be discussed. Top of the line in the field, William Hobé came from a long line of jewelry makers in France. His designs were intense and impeccable. He worked on the belief that quality need not be neglected in an affordable piece of jewerly. By the 1940s he was Hollywoods sweetheart, designing many pieces for the stars. The craftsmanship of a Hobe piece is unmistakable. Trademarks used by the company were "Jewels by Hobé" and then "Jewels of Legendary Splendor". Not easily found on the market today an early Hobé piece is a true find. The company today is a major thrust in the costume jewelry world and maintains a tremendous standard of excellence.

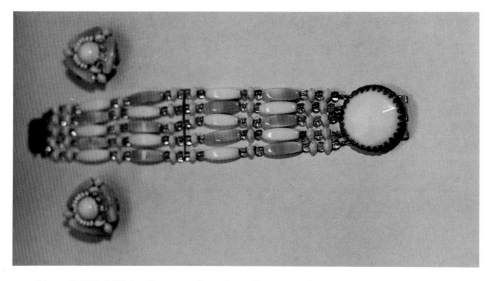

Signed "Hobé" 3-piece set showing glass polished stones in whites and lavendar, earrings are clip-ons, c. 1950—$85.

In 1985 the name of Miriam Haskell could be heard echoing from one dealer to another. Right now Haskell Jewelry Ltd. is most desirable on the market. The company was founded by Miriam Haskell a yesteryears womans libber whose designs in jewelry were accepted as soon as they hit the market. Today the company continues the traits of its founder under the tutelage of Mr. Sanford G. Moss. Even today the jewelry produced by the company is hand assembled and quality and originality continues to abound.

Miriam Haskell ear-
rings, gold with cinne-
bar drops (screw-on).
Value $25. Hobé
bracelet of heavy silver
mesh with center
design and safety
chain. Value $95.
Hobé earrings, clip-
on mauve moonstone
with irridescent beads.
Value $15.

Miriam Haskell signed pieces including bracelet
with silver wash, showing Peking glass beads and
crystals with safety clasp. Value $65. Pin has gold
wash. Value $30

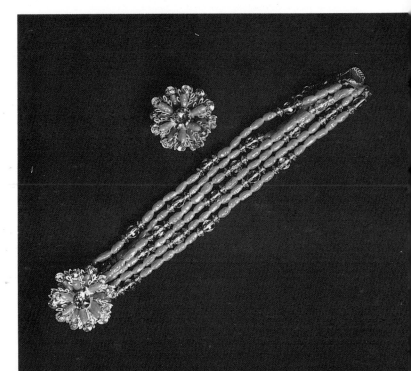

Hattie Carnegie simulated jade on brushed gold pin, c. 1950. Value $45.

Hattie Carnegie Jewelry was another high fashion look that entered the costume jewelry world with a splash. In retrospect the design and materials used were not as awe inspiring as Haskell or Hobé yet Carnegie pieces are still being collected and with a little searching can still be found at local flea markets, antique stores and house sales.

If some of the previous companies discussed represent the top of the line in costume jewelry or fashion jewelry, Trifari represents the entire industry as a whole. Dealing from the top of the line and fashion jewelry down to filling the wants and desires of the average woman with jewels of fine quality for moderate prices. Trifari is filled with a history of strong leadership, great designers, quality goods and a wonderful understanding of the times. This company may be viewed as the epitomy of the industry.

Since 1924 Trifari, Krussman and Fishel has been producing a fine line of costume jewelry and setting the pace for much of the industry. Gus Trifari and Leo Krussman had been in their own rhinestone business since 1918. In 1924 they took in a new partner Carl Fishel who had been a vice president of a hair ornament and comb company. With Fishel in sales and Trifari and Krussman in design the company was off to a great start. By 1930 the company had added to its staff Alfred Philippe a top French designer. Philippe, noted for his animal designs and moveable jewelry took the lead in costume designing in America.

By 1939 the company had moved to East Providence, Rhode Island with their show room remaining in New York City. Weathering well through creativity during the war years, Trifari came into the 50s as a leader in better costume jewelry. It has been reported that not only did Trifari design for Broadway shows but also had Sophie Tucker strutting their rhinestones. Trifari even went to the White House in the 50s with Mamie Eisenhower who had the company design a pearl necklace for the Inaugural Ball. Four years later Trifari once again assisted the first lady with another necklace for the Ball. Both of these pieces were displayed at the Smithsonian Institute's Bicentennial exhibit of first ladies inaugural gowns in the Hall of Science and Industry.

Three piece set done by Trifari in 1954. The company put out a run of 10,000 pieces each. Earrings were sold for $4, bracelet $6 and necklace $10. Finish on back as good as front, a trademark of Trifari.

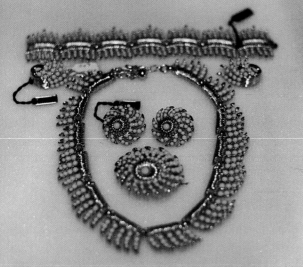

Trifari turquoise sets put out in 1957 consisting of a two piece bracelet and earring set and a three piece necklace, earring and pin set. Value $50 and $75 respectively.

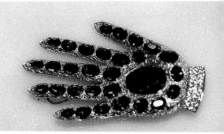

Magnificent hand done by Trifari in 1946 using Austrian rhinestones. Sold in 1946 for $40. Value $125.

Flower pin of turquoise and gold also made to be used on a chain. Value $15. Flower pin, brushed gold with coral and rhinestones. Value $15. Necklace of brushed gold leaves. Value $20. Necklace of gold and white. Value $15.

In 1975, the Hallmark Cards, Inc., acquired Trifari and the tradition of quality continued. The company today enjoys a fine reputation in fashion jewelry and remains one of the top contenders and trend setters in the industry. Today collectors, due to the abundance of merchandise put out by Trifari, can still find good pieces. The trademark to look for is the Trifari crown. In business now for over 61 years Trifari represents some of the best of the Industry that took this country by storm.

Three piece mother of pearl and rhinestone set done by Trifari in 1958. Stones done in pastel pinks, yellows and greens. Value $65.

Trifari 3 piece sea-flower set goldtone base studded with pearls seen on the market in 1951. Value $35.

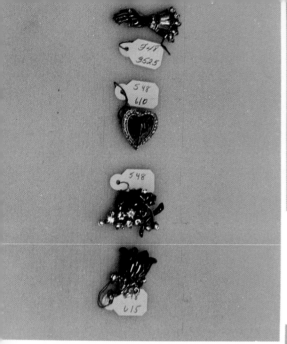

Novelty pins displaying multi-colored rhinestones and pearls, all wheels on pins are moveable. Finish is 30 years old and still brilliant. Trifari, 1956. Value $20 each.

Novelty pins put out by Trifari in 1948. All demonstrate use of rhinestones. Value $20 each.

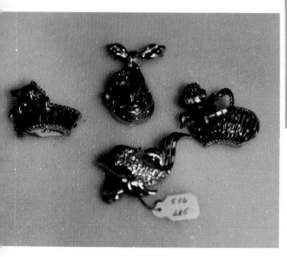

Election animal pins—put out by Trifari in 1948. Sold were 1,125 donkeys and 1,350 elephants.

Novelty pins of 1956 by Trifari showing 2 dog pins, a cat in a basket and a fish pin. All pins done in brushed gold and rhinestones. Value $20 each.

REAL VS. IMITATION

The history of glass can be traced far back in time to both Egypt and China. In both of these realms glass was often used as an imitator for gem stones. The Chinese even used glass at times to ape their most precious gem jade. By the 19th century once again we have seen that glass with the aid of new technology and the addition of lead to its content, was used to imitate the diamond.

By the twentieth century with the advent of synthetic or man-made stones, glass was everywhere in the jewelry industry. What must be remembered is that early in the history of costume jewelry often glass was set in precious metals. With this in mind it is important to understand some ways to tell glass from gemstones.

Although extensive testing is often accomplished with complicated equipment, basic testing can be done with a magnifying glass and good light. As far as an image being seen through the stone, diamond when looked through in a good light will show a clear image. Gemstones will also show an image but not as clearly as the diamond. Once one is dealing with glass, the image will be distorted due to the softness of the glass and the inability to achieve a perfect polish. Coldness may also be used to help judge glass from gemstones. If put to the lips, the gemstone will be colder to the touch than will the glass.

Since diamonds and gemstones are harder than glass look carefully with a magnifying glass or loop for signs of wear. Scratches and jeweler tool marks on the stones indicate glass because of its softness. Still another test to aid in indication is that of color testing. Real stones tend to have areas of more concentrated color. Called zoning by the trade, these hot spots of color are not present in synthetics or glass where color is uniform throughout the stones.

Air bubbles are still another clue to the authenticity of a stone. Glass will definitely show air bubbles when looked through with a loop. Gas bubbles may also be evident. This is caused by the heating process used. In glass, these bubbles will look like cavities or spheres. Precious stones have no air or gas bubbles present.

The cut of a stone may also help tell real from imitation. Due to the properties of gemstones, cutting is often irregular. The synthetic stone or glass often display uniform and precise cuts for being softer, it is easier to cut.

AMBER

Amber is an organic material that will change color with age. Ranging from shades of yellow, thru cherry red to dark browns it is found in the Baltic regions. One of the earliest forms of decoration, amber remained popular all thru the 1920s and into the thirties. With the advent of plastics, amber was copied and at times is difficult to tell.

The hot needle test may give two evidences in detecting amber. First if a hot needle is applied to amber a pine smell should be emitted and along with this smell should be seen a white smoke. If the amber is plastic, the needle heat should leave signs of melting. This test is by no means perfect for imitation Russian amber contains small amounts of real amber and may give of the same pine smell and white smoke.

Amber for its size is exceedingly light weight, so that if you are holding a heavy piece of amber, further testing needs to be done. If amber is placed in a salt solution, the real will float while the imitation normally sinks to the bottom. These are interesting tests but if any doubt remains a reputable jeweler should be consulted.

Amber glass beads 8" long with early clasp, c. 1930. Value $25. Plastic amber color earrings, c. 1950. Value $10.

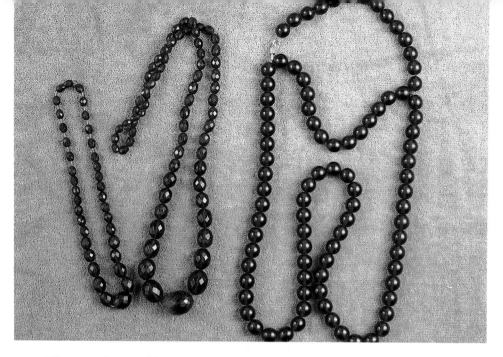

Three amber necklaces representing the turn of the century. L. to R. short restrung faceted and graduated amber with yellow glass spacers. $150. Hand faceted red Baltic Amber on chain demonstrating graduated amber. $300. Bib type red cherry Baltic amber with 14k gold clasp. $350.

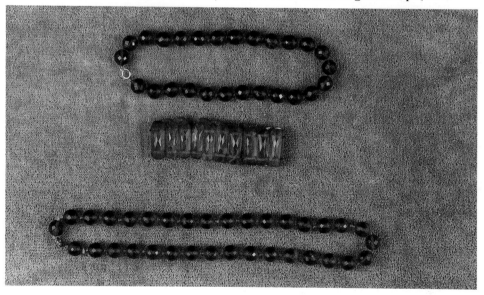

Short necklace of red amber, turn of the century, value $125. Lighter amber necklace, hand knotted, $125. Center piece an amber bracelet made of melted and reformed amber. Clue to melting is crystalized appearance. Value $45.

JET

Fashionable during the Victorian age and down through the 20s and 30s with some resurgence later on, jet is often confused with gutta percha and black jet onyx and even black glass beads. Often people may even confuse plastic beads with this fossil form. One thing to remember when checking for jet is that it is very lightweight. Another test, however extremely expensive, is to rub the jet across an abrasive material such as concrete. When this procedure is used a blackish, brownish line should be left on the concrete. It is advisable before this step is taken to consult, once again, a reputable jeweler.

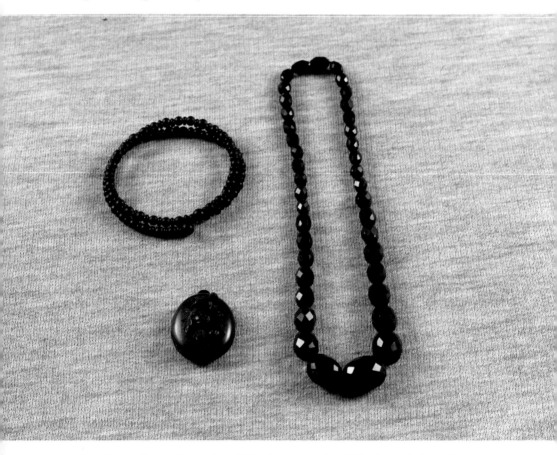

Jet—popular up into the 1920s, jet is a resin, light in weight and warm to the touch and looks dull compared to its imitator black glass. Bracelet showing jet balls and jet spacers, c. 1870-1900. Value $40. Jet mourning locket, used to carry lock of hair. Value $50. Necklace, self clasped in jet, 6" strand showing graduated faceted beads strung with black thread, c. 1910. Value $75.

JADE AND IVORY

With the influence of the Orient manifesting itself in the late 20s and 30s, both jade and ivory became important in jewelry design. Jade, coming in various forms itself and being such a precious commodity should be thoroughly tested by a jeweler not only for whether it is fake or not but for its quality as jade itself. Both slivers of glass and plastic have been used to imitate this gem of the east.

Elephant Ivory used by the Chinese for centuries to produce jewelry is often imitated in the 20th century due to modern technology and the use of plastic. Ivory may take the form today of wax, celluloid or plastic. Elephant ivory may be identified by weight, a mellow color that will darken with age and by what appears to be parallel lines in the grain or in cross section zig-zag lines. The new plastics however can copy ivory very well even down to the lines. The hot needle test will show plastic however as well as a careful look for mold marks and seams.

Imitation jade type stones with clasp marked Japan. 28" strand individually knotted, c. 1920s. Value $45.

PEARLS

Pearls down through the ages have been used in jewelry and continued to hold a strong place through the 20th century. The use of imitation pearls is not a new phenomenon but dates back to France and a french rosary maker by the name of Jacquin. The process he formulated was used until the 20th century.[3] A hollow sphere of glass was lined with a fish scale mixture which gave the bead a pearly look. Then the inside was filled with wax.

Today there are two tests used for telling real from imitation pearls. The first deals with the string holes on the pearl. Check carefully for signs of a film over glass at the drill hole. The second test that is tried and true is to rub a string of pearls over ones teeth. If real, they should feel gritty to the touch, if imitation the rubbing will be smooth.

Pearls—Pair of wrap around bracelets, color running from taupes to off whites to gray whites. Lustre brighter than real pearls, c. 1940s. Value $10 each. Simulated pearl necklace in the Baroque manner. Color ranges from pink to irridescent, c. 1920. Value $30. Floral pearl decoration on chain, c. 1930s. Value $35.

Signed "De Mario" 3 strand pearl necklace and matching pin. Necklace displays hand set rhinestones as spacers. Value $50.

Gold necklace and matching pin set. Pendant showing large center cabochon surrounded by pearls. Pin features hand set rhinestones and pearls. Value $20 necklace, $18 pin.

Hand carved mother of pearl necklace and pendant, carving well done, c. 1960s. Value $35.

"La Rachelle' Pearls, mother of pearl choker with original guarantee for indestructibility. C. 1920 Value $45.

DATING

In testing, one uses many senses, including sight, feel, and smell to detect the real or unreal commodity. The dating of costume jewelry is not as exacting a science as testing. Styles as we have seen changed rapidly and often reappeared years down the line. Much of the fun in collecting costume is to try to fix a time period to a piece, this however is not always a success. The knowledge of times and trends in dress and society will indeed help in the quest but is not always the answer. Even the costume jewelry industry up until the 50s was lax in their cataloging of styles and trends in jewelry.

Costume jewelry, whether collected to be worn, framed, or put back in the cardboard box where it may have just came from, is a wide open field, one that can be entered with little trepidation and a lot of fun. The nostalgia of the twentieth century lives through these little bits of glitter and what better way to tell the tale.

NECKLACES

Phyllis Originals: three piece set of prong set rhinestones. Necklace, choker type with safety chain. Bracelet with safety chain. Earrings, square shape, screw-on. Value $75 for set.

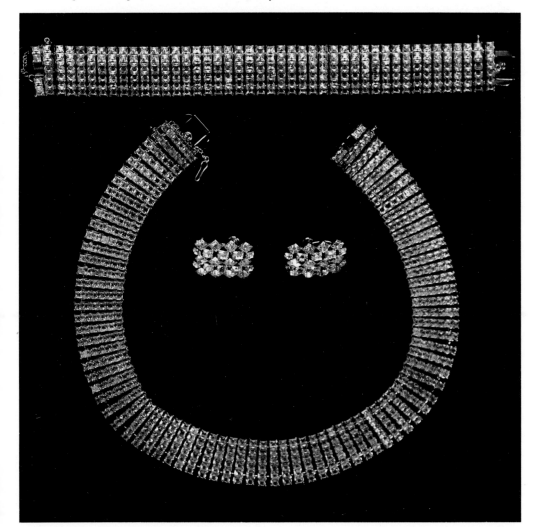

Three examples of the 1920s from l. to r. Garnet colored crystals 18", pink glass faceted bead and jet type faceted beads with rondells. Value $30-$45.

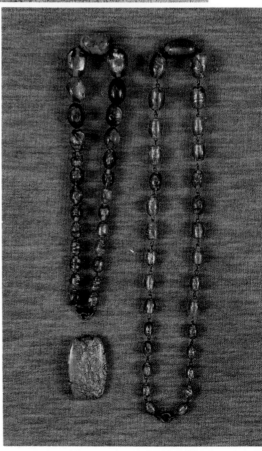

Gold Foil Jewelry—popular in the 1920s necklace showing graduated gold foil glass beads. Value $20. Long necklace of foil beads on chain. Value $30. Gold foil pin with early clasp. Value $15.

Unusual brilliance in hand set rhinestones and iridescences. Choker shows a Deco design, c. 1930s. Value $45.

Multi shades of pink to red polished glass stones displayed well in 3 piece set, c. 1950. Value $45.

Iridescent necklace with gold backing, rhinestones hand set in style of the 40s. Value $45. Floral cluster pin hand set stones in a zig-zag pattern, c. 1950s. Value $20. Bracelet with iridescent and blue emerald cut rhinestones, c. 1940s. Value $25. Screw on earrings, c. 1940s. Value $15. Cluster of beads mounted for brooch showing aurora borealis, c. 1950s. Value $15.

4 piece rhinestone and blue polished stone set. All hand set, earrings displaying screw-on-backs. Setting all rhodium finishes, c. 1950s. Value $125.

Lady Princess Crown Jewels. Three piece set. Yellow glass leaves in gold colored setting with amber colored rhinestones pasted in each leaf. $65 for set.

Glass beads with rhinestones on chain, excellent design and craftsmanship, c. 1930s. Value $55.

Tomas—Exquisite design. Three piece set; necklace of green square stones in scalloped silver setting with links of pasted set rhinestones. Bracelet with safety chain. Clip-on earrings. $75 for set.

Trifari collection. Signed on clasp "Trifari" necklace with handset rhinestones, c. 1950s. Value $65. Brushed gold "Trifari" signed necklace with hand set pink rhinestones, c. 1950s. Value $65. Spray pin in brushed gold, delicate leaf pattern, stamped "Trifari", c. late 50s. Value $45. Red cabochon stones form this signed "Trifari" necklace with an extension clasp for a longer look, c. 1930s. Value $45.

Weiss collection shows exceptional settings and stones. Top to bottom: Large star shaped pin displaying amber multi-faceted rhinestones with smokey colored smaller rhinestones all hand set. Piece signed "Weiss" on back center of mount, c. 1950s. Value $45. Christmas tree pin, brushed green on gold with colored rhinestones pasted in setting showing "Weiss" mark, c. 1950s. Value $15. Clip-on earrings marked "Weiss" featuring rhinestones in amber and red, c. 1950s. Value $15. Circular brooch with amber colored rhinestones, hand set marked "Weiss" on mount, c. 1940-1950. Value $15-$20. Iridescent rhinestone hand set necklace with gold backing signed "Weiss". This piece displays great workmanship and sense of design, c. 1950. Value $50.

Crystal Beads—fashionable in the 1920s—Red glass made in Danzig with self contained barrel clasp, graduated and faceted beads. Value $35. Clear crystals with pink spacers on chain with a sterling clasp. Value $40. Clear crystal with multi-faceted beads showing white glass spacers and sterling clasp. Value $40. Clear crystal with five large beads on chain showing sterling clasp. Value $45. Amber color glass faceted beads with flat bottoms. Value $45.

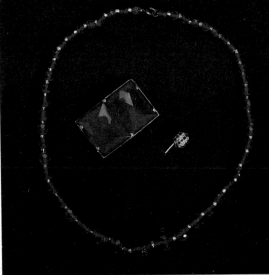

Red crystal beads, multi-faceted. Value $20. Buckle of prong set red glass. Value $10. Antique stick pin of red, white and blue prong set stones. Value $35.

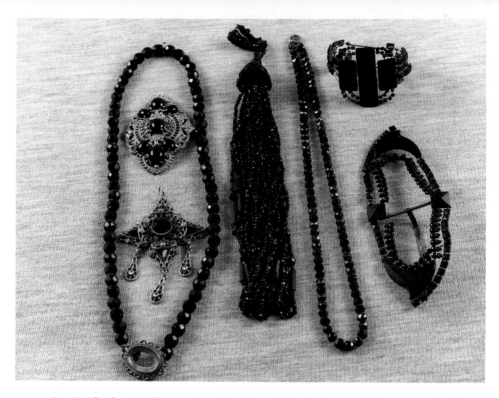

Basic Black—Both strands of beads are black glass and differ from jet in being much heavier, shinier and colder to the touch, c. 1920s. Value $45 each. Cabochon stones set in marcasite pin, c. 1930s. Value $30. Pendant showing black glass faceted stones, c. 1930s. Value $25. Decorative tassel from 1920s belt. Tassel is made up of black glass beads. Value $25. Black beads on wire unusual piece indeed along with a black glass beaded belt buckle with brass hook, c. 1910. Value $35.

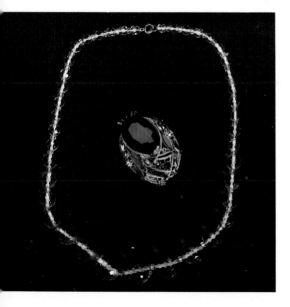

Blue crystal beads, multi-faceted. Value $20. Oval pin of blue and red prong set stones, signed Art Co. Value $15.

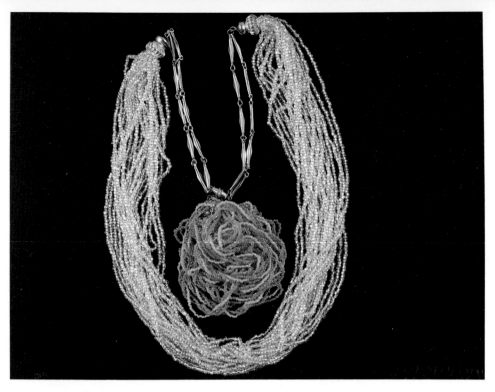

Heavy silver beaded necklace fashioned after the "Flapper" era showing barrel clasp on silver chain, c. 1950s. Value $45. Multi-colored blue glass beads, rope style made in Italy, c. 1940. Value $25.

Baubles—necklace, bracelet and earrings made up of glass balls on chain. Earrings are marked sterling, c. 1920. Value of set $45.

Two piece set. Necklace with white iridescent stones, prong set with matching clip-on earrings. Value $25.

Bakelite link necklace with gold medallions, 20"long, c. 1930s. Value $50.

Triple chain necklace and large painted enamel floral pendant with four large hand set rhinestones. Value $22.

PLASTICS

Signed "Alexis Kirk", long strand of beads of triangular plastic with pewter side piece. Value $35. Twisted bangle bracelet with elephant figural. Value $15.

Art deco by Lady Princess. Three piece set. Light and dark blue plastic pasted on 24k gold plate necklace on chain. Value $65 for set.

Vendome, chunky plastic three piece set. Hot pink and green necklace with stretch bracelet and screw-on earrings. Value $65 for set.

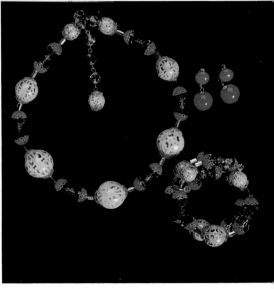

Trifari gold beaded 3 strand necklace and matching bracelet. Pieces show exceptional craftsmanship. These types of goods sold mostly in jewelry stores rather than department stores, c. 1950s. Value $125.

Large floral plastic pin with hand set varigated pink rhinestones, c. 1950s. Value $15. Modern plastic necklace by "Isadora" featuring large molded flowers, c. 1979. Value $25.

Plastic graduated 3 strand beads with matching button earrings, c. 1950s. Value $25 set.

BRACELETS AND PINS

Signed Florenza set featuring blue enamel and seed pearl. Set shows clip-on earrings and safety clasp on bracelet. Pin also has hook to connect to necklace. Value $50 for set.

Late 1940s plastic bracelet. Value $15-$25. Also pictured, Rhodium plate leaf motif lapel pin with foil backed rhinestones, green on green, c. 1940s. Value $25.

From top to bottom, Signed "Van Dell" 1/12 gold filled floral pin, c. 1950s. Value $10. Signed "Trifari" rhinestone pin, c. 1950s. Value $30. Signed "Listner" turquoise and amber bow pin, c. 1950s. Value $20. Signed "Coro" bracelet with hand set stones and a rhodium base, c. 1940s. Value $25.

Multi-faceted red glass bracelet marked "Kinney, Providence Rhode Island." Value $25.

Two piece set, floral pin and earrings. Black enamel flowers with green leaves. Signed "Coro". Value $15. Bracelet of black stone with prong set rhinestones. Value $35. Butterfly pin, signed "Trifari" of black enamel and gold. Value $15. Floral pin, brushed on gold with prong set black stones and rhinestones. Value $10.

Wide Wide World
Assortment of wide bracelets in clear rhinestones showing multi-faceted center stones in diamond and emerald cuts. Top piece signed "Weiss", c. 1920s-30s. Value $95 each.

Collection of Italian mosaic jewelry, bracelets, scatter pins, novelty pins and clip on earrings. Jewelry formed by using small pieces of stone plastered into setting to form designs. Popular in the 20s and 30s. Value $10-$30.

Butterflys
Blue butterfly, good stones, prong set. Value $15. Signed pink and red Florenza spring mounted butterfly with moveable wings. Value $25. Butterflies on right demonstrate enamel, rhinestones and smokey glass stones. Value $15 each.

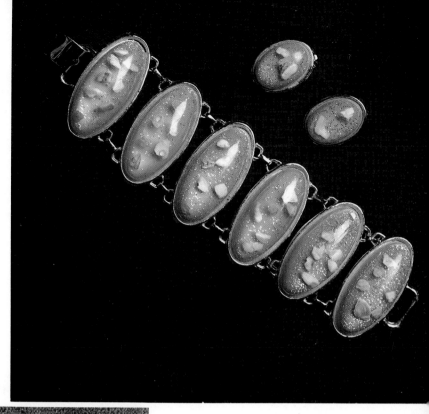

Bracelet and earring set showing encased shells on pink gold flecked background, c. 1950s. Value $40.

Grouping of "Weiss" pieces all signed. Weiss known for fine work in rhinestones. Goldtone bracelet dates to 1950s. Value $30. Clear rhinestone drop earrings with clasp back. Late 40s-50s. Value $35. Lower right is stamped pin with multi-sized rhinestones pasted in setting, 1950s. Value $25.

"Flowers"

Top, clockwise: Signed "Weiss" novelty pin showing enamel on brushed gold. Daisy with lady bug, c. 1950s. Value $15. Brushed gold on sterling floral pin, signed "Coro", with amber rhinestones in center. Value $30. Signed BSN gold wash floral pin with orange and white seed pearls. Value $25. Rhinestone spray pin, prong set multi-faceted stones. Value 25. Signed "Weiss" enamel floral pin with caboshon stones. Value $20.

Center: signed "Trifari" orange enamel leaf with rhinestones on stem and bug. Value $45.

Fun Stuff
Top to bottom, left to right: "Coro" dragon fly, gold wash on sterling
with multi-colored prong set stones. Value $25. Indian princess, gold
colored with dangle chains and pink stone eyes. Value $10. Indian head
pin, black dull enamel on gold metal with pasted rhinestones on band.
Eyes of red stones. Value $10. Gold colored bumble bee with turquoise
stones. Value $10. Black brushed enamel panda bear. Pasted rhinestones,
red stone eyes and moveable head. Value $35. Owl on perch with
brushed gold, pasted rhinestones and green stone eyes. Value $10.

Sterling pins—Top left pin is an unusual chrysanthemum with falling petals, c. 1930s Value $45. Two pins next to chrysanthemum pin also 1930s valued $15 and $20 respectively. Bottom two pins are much thinner in composition, c. 1950s. Value $15.

Cut steel, heart shaped belt buckle, c. 1920s. Value $25.

Popular butterfly pin with autumn color rhinestones. Stones pasted in setting, c. 1950s. Value $10.

Novelty Pins—Late 1940s and 1950s showing figural birds, flowers, wishbone and sword. All demonstrating the use of rhinestones. Value $10-$20.

Collection of rhinestone and colored glass dress clips from the 1930s and 1940s. Value $10-$20.

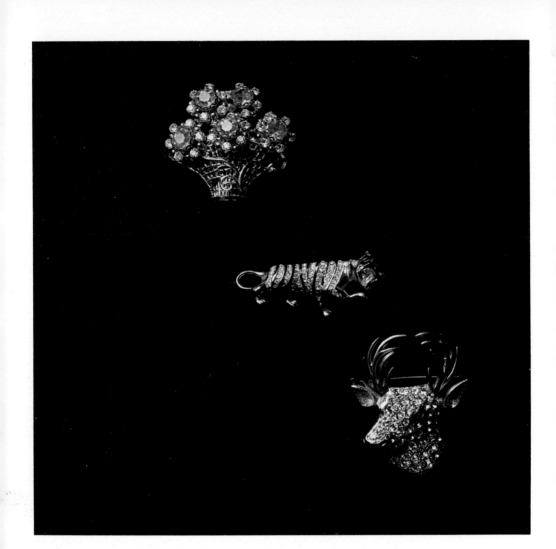

Floral bouquet pin with clear and yellow rhinestones. Tiger pin with brushed gold and set in rhinestones. Signed "Ora". Deer head pin, set in gold showing pasted rhinestones. Each pin $25.

Large flowering cactus pin with rhinestones mounted on brush gold leaves, c. 1960s. Value $40. Rhinestone spray pin, c. 1950s with prong set rhinestones. Value $20. Austrian pin with faceted hand set rhinestones. Value $25.

Multi-colored rhinestone novelty pins all from the 1950's, some demonstrating moveable parts. Value $15-$25.

Signed "Trifari" pin with Deco influence. Demonstrating green rhinestones with gold brush finish. Design and workmanship well done, c. 1950s. Value $20.

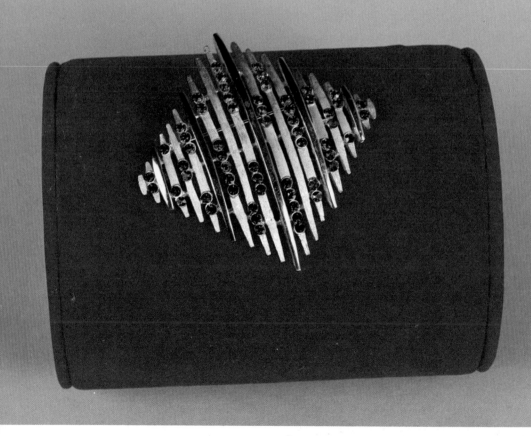

Signed "Weiss" coral and amber color hand set rhinestone pin. Stone shapes that of pear and round. Value $20.

Signed "Emmons" silver filigree large floral pin with safety catch. Value $15.

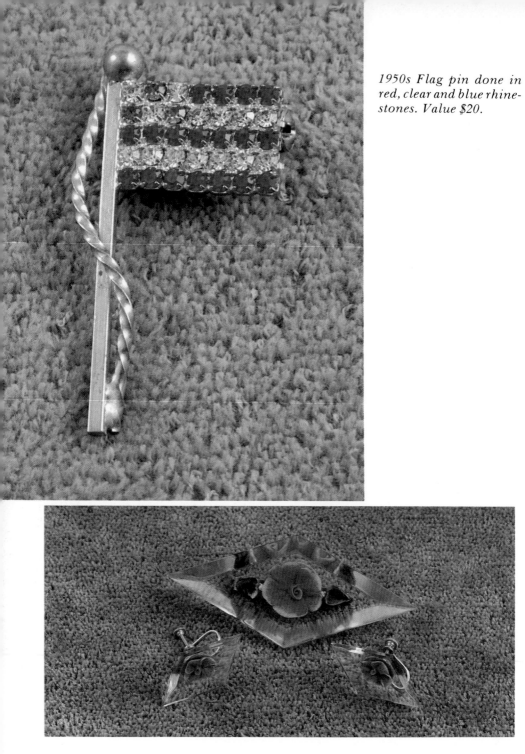

1950s Flag pin done in red, clear and blue rhinestones. Value $20.

Lucite pin with matching earrings, c. 1940s. Value $20.

Art Deco dress clip with large simulated aqua marine stones and clear rhinestones, larger stones hand set, c. 1930s. Value $25.

Merry Christmas
Top to bottom, left to right: Signed "Weiss" Christmas tree pin, brushed green gold with pasted rhinestones. Signed "Weiss" Christmas bells pin, brushed gold with enameled green leaves, moveable red bead clappers and matching clip-on earrings. Leaf pin with enameled green leaves with flowers of pasted rhinestones and clip-on earrings to match. Signed "Weiss" Christmas ornament pin, red brushed on gold with pasted colored stones and matching clip-on earrings. Signed "Weiss" Christmas tree pin with pasted multi-colored stones. Christmas tree pin of brushed gold with pasted rhinestones.

Top to bottom, left to right: Poodle pin of brushed gold with dangle chains and red stone eyes. Value $10. Pair of cockatoos, gold and silver colored. Pasted rhinestones on wings and crest, red stone eyes. Value $15. Pair of horse scatter pins by "Marvella". Brushed gold with genuine pearl. Value $25. Brushed gold owl of pasted rhinestones. Value $10.

Figural Fun—Strawberry pin with black enamel base, c. late 1950s. Value $15. Sailor boy, perhaps Buster Brown, glass amber beads and metal body, c. 1930. Value $25. Brass enamelled grasshopper on a branch signed Spain, c. 1950. Value $15. Marcasite peacock on base metal with rhinestones, c. 1930s. Value $35. Rhinestone bee with purple cabochons hand set, c. 1950s. Value $20. Strawberry scatter pins from the 60s and clip on strawberry earrings from the 50s. Value $5 on pins, $10 on earrings.

Amethyst rhinestone pin, well made with prong setting, c. 1940s. $25. Matching amethyst color stones, prong set with filigree work. $15.

Flower pin, brushed gold with light and deep purple prong set stones. Value $25. Pin with blue and rose colored prong set stones. Value $25. Crescent pin, signed "Kramer" with multi-colored prong set stones on gold metal. Value $25.

Flower cluster pin of white enamel with multi-colored prong set stones.
Value $25. Bar type pin with red and pink prong set stones. Value $20.
Pin with gold filigree, shades of pink prong set stones. Value $25.

Stick Pins—popular at turn of the century for mens neckties, soon adapted by women for lapels and scarves. Collection here ranges from Austrian opal in Matrix to cats eyes, to amethyst, sterling, and glass c. 1900-1930s. Value $10 to $85.

ACCESSORIES

Bags—Art Deco colored mess bag, probably of French origin, c. 1920s. Value $45. Black and silver beaded bag, displaying a Deco motif, c. late 20s. Value $25. "Whiting Davis" mess bag and change purse signed "Silver Soldered Mess" with blue stone clasp on purse, c. 1930. Value purse $55, change purse $35. c. 1950s. "Whiting Davis" purse. Value $25.

Belt buckles—two rhinestone belt buckles, c. 1920s. Value $15. Art Deco plastic belt buckle with metal backing, c. 1930. Value $15.

Plastic and rhinestone belt buckle, c. 1920. Value $30.

Notes

CHAPTER 1: JEWELRY HISTRONICS
[1] J. Anderson Black, *The Story of Jewelry* (New York: William Morrow and Company Inc., 1974), 84.
[2] J. Anderson Black, 69-71.
[3] Mona Curran, *A Treasury of Jewels and Gemstones* (New York: Emerson Books Inc., 1961), 61.
[4] Curran, *A Treasury of Jewels and Gemstones*, 63.
[5] Black, *The Story of Jewelry*, 53.

CHAPTER 2: TRENDS AND INFLUENCES 1920-70
[1] David Saville Muzzey, *A History of Our Country* (New York: Ginn and Company, 1955), 533.
[2] " 'My Lady's Dress' is Bow Reformed", New York Times, 25 June 1921, p.6.
[3] "Ridicule Moral Gown" New York Times, 16 February, 1921.
[4] Isabelle M. Archer, "The Jewelry of 1926," The Jewelers' Circular, 3 February, 1926.
[5] "Mme. Chanel" New York Times, 15 March, 1931, sec.9.
[6] Jeanenne Bell, *Old Jewelry Second Edition* (Alabama: Books Americana, 1985), 245.
[7] "Jewelry Sales Aid Chinese War Orphans" New York Times, 4 October, 1939, p. 11.
[8] Bell, *Old Jewelry Second Edition*, 307.
[9] "Costume Jewelry Shows Femininity" New York Times, 24 June , 1947, p. 31.
[10] "Chalk Beads Rival Pearls in Style" New York Times, 30 March, 1949.
[11] "More Selectivity in Spring Ordering" New York Times, 20 November, 1949, Sec. III, p.6.
[12] "Dollar Jewelry is Still Popular" New York Times, 8 November, 1955, p.49.

CHAPTER 3: A WORD ABOUT...
[1] M.D.S. Lewis, *Antique Paste Jewellry*, (London: Faber and Faber, 1970), 17.
[2] Maryanne Dolan, *Collecting Rhinestone Jewelry*, (Alabama: Books Americana, 1984), 25.
[3] M.D.S. Lewis, *Antique Paste Jewellry*, 76.

Bibliography

Baker, Lilian. *100 Years of Collectible Jewelry*. Kentucky: Collector Books, 1978.

———, *Fifty Years of Collectible Fashion Jewelry 1925-1975*. Kentucky: Collector Books, 1986.

Black, J. Anderson. *The Story of Jewelry*. New York: William Morrow and Company, Inc., 1974.

Bell, Jeanenne. *Answers to Questions About Old Jewelry 1840-1950*. Alabama: Books Americana, 1985.

Coarelli, Filippo. *Greek and Roman Jewellery*. London: Hamlyn Publishing Group, 1970.

Curran, Mona. *A Treasury of Jewels and Gemstones*. New York: Emerson Books, Inc., 1961.

Chu, Arthur and Grace. *Oriental Antiques and Collectibles, A Guide*. New York: Crown Publishers, Inc., 1973.

———, *The Collector's Book of Jade*. New York: Crown Publishers, Inc., 1978.

Dolan, Maryanne. *Collecting Rhinestone Jewelry*. Alabama: Books Americana, Inc., 1984.

Heichelheim, Fritz M. and Yeo, Cedric. *A History of the Roman People*. New Jersey: Prentice-Hall, Inc., 1962.

Henzel, Sylvia, S. *Collectible Costume Jewelry*. Illinois: Wallace-Homestead, 1982.

Jenkins, Alan. *The Thirties*. London: Stein and Day, 1976.

Lewis, M.D.S. *Antique Paste Jewellery*. London: Faber and Faber, 1970.

Matlins, Antoinette Leonard, and Bonanno, Antonio C. *The Complete Guide to Buying Gems*. New York: Crown Publishers, Inc., 1984.

Moss, H. St. L.B. *The Birth of the Middle Ages 395-814*. New York: Oxford University Press, 1964.

Muzzey, David Saville. *A History of Our Country*. Boston: Ginn and Company, 1955.

Sataloff, Joseph and Richards, Allison. *The Pleasure of Jewelry and Gemstones*. London: Octopus Books Limited, 1975.

Steingraber, Erich. *Antique Jewelry*. New York: Frederich A. Praeger: Publishers, 1957.

PERIODICALS, JOURNALS, MAGAZINES AND CATALOGUES

Archer, Isabelle. "A forecast of the Jewelry for 1921." The Jewelers' Circular, vol. LXXXII No. 1, Feb. 2, 1921, 147-154.

———, "A Forecast of the Jewelry for 1922." The Jewelers' Circular, vol. LXXXIV No. 1, Feb. 1922, 113-122.

———, "A Forecast of the Jewelry of 1923." The Jewelers' Circular, vol. LXXXVI No. 1, Feb., 1923. 107-115.

———, "What Jewelry Will Be Worn in 1924." The Jewelers' Circular, vol. LXXXVII No. 1, Feb., 1924. 113-125.

———, "The Features of the Jewelry of 1925". The Jewelers' Circular Vol. XC Feb., 1925.

———, "A Forecast of Jewelry of 1928." The Jewelers' Circular, Feb. 1928, 102-107.

Baird-North Co., Catalogues. 1927, 1930.

Books of Gems, Royal Diamond and Watch Co., 1931.

Jewelers' Circular, Feb. 1926.

New York Times. Jan.25, 1921, p.6. Feb. 28, 1921. Nov. 26, 1922, p.14. Nov. 28, 1922, p.14. Feb 3, 1928. January 20, 1931. March 15, 1931, sec.9. p.6. July 5, 1931. Jan. 26, 1933. Feb. 7, 1933. May 7, 1933. Nov. 24, 1933. Nov. 25, 1933. Feb. 23, 1936. August 15, 1937. March 18, 1939. Dec. 8, 1940, p.7. Jan. 4, 1941, p.20. April 6, 1941, p.13. May 16, 1941, p.32. June 28, 1941, p.22. Jan. 24, 1942, p.20. March 25, 1942, p.33. April 7, 1942, p.12. April 8, 1942, p.27. April 18, 1942, p.27. July 2, 1942, p.30. July 12, 1942, Feb. 8, 1943, p.43. April 17, 1943. Feb. 5, 1944, p.11. May 5, 1944. June 21, 1944, p.28. Sept. 14, 1945, p.17. Aug. 15, 1946, p.31-36. Feb. 10, 1947, p.34. Aug.13, 1947. Jan. 2, 1948, p.50. Feb. 6, 1948, p.38. June 8, 1948, p.20. Dec. 1, 1948, p.38. Feb. 3, 1949, p.36. Feb. 25, 1949. March 6, 1949, March 30, 1949. June 11, 1949. June 28, 1949, p.44. July 12, 1949, p.32. Nov. 30, 1949. Jan. 19, 1950, p.34. Feb. 18, 1950, p.10. July 10, 1950, p.24. July 13, 1950. Oct. 29, 1950, p.40-1. March 31, 1951. Nov. 4, 1951, p.8. Jan. 2, 1952. June 25, 1952, p.32. May 12, 1953, p.43. March 23, 1954, p.22. March 29, 1954, p.33. Nov. 8, 1955, p.49. Aug. 16, 1958, sec. III p.1.

Schifter, Jim. "Quality Jewelry since 1924". Crown Magazine, Oct. 1976.

The Noon News, Nov. 15, 1955, Dec. 3, 1985.

The Rambler. "A forecast of Jewelry for 1920". The Jewelers' Circular, vol. LXXX. Feb., 1920. 145-152.

Thompson, Irma. "A Review of the Styles in Jewelry of the Past Year." The Jewelers' Circular, Feb. 1922. 137-47.

Vogue Magazine, Sept. 15, 1961.